Praise for
Tamar

"If you enjoy squeezing every delicious drop of truth from the stories found in Scripture, Shadia Hrichi's new study on Tamar will delight you. She handles God's Word with exceeding care, pointing us to the many vital lessons worth learning and applying to our own lives. As a Bible teacher, I especially appreciate the options she offers small groups, from a light or moderate time commitment to in-depth or all-in. As an all-in woman, I love the depth and breadth of the questions to consider, the Bible verses to ponder, the word studies to review, and the compassionate unfolding of Tamar's story. When you go *Behind the Seen* with Shadia, you are in very good hands!"

—**Liz Curtis-Higgs,** best-selling author of *Bad Girls of the Bible*

"After going through Shadia's Bible study on Hagar, I couldn't wait to see what she would do next. *Tamar* is another outstanding Bible study, rich in historical detail, cultural insights, and applicable life lessons for us today. I appreciate Shadia sharing personal stories from her own life (some heartbreaking, some amusing), which help shine light on Tamar's story. Perfect for personal and/or group study."

—**Francine Rivers,** international best-selling author

"If you embark on a Shadia Hrichi Bible study, know that you are in good hands. I love how she talks directly to you, cheering you on and giving you previews of the road ahead. It's comforting! And when you study the story of Tamar from the book of Genesis, you will want comfort for this challenging story of a woman with a very unique role in biblical history. In *Tamar*, you will get to know a woman who faced a very difficult and painful path. The experts debate her choices and her motivations, but there seems to be a strong and lasting faith in God and his promises that underlies her actions. Ultimately, she gives birth to an ancestor of Jesus and is forever (and intentionally) memorialized in the genealogy of the Messiah. I don't want to give away the story, or the stories of Shadia's own difficult life woven together with Tamar's. For that, you'll need to dive into this study yourself, and even better, with a group of friends. Tamar's life altered the trajectory of human history, and this very engaging study will put those pieces together for you in this powerful picture of God at work in the midst of a mess. Highly recommended."

—**Susy Flory,** *New York Times* best-selling author and coauthor, and director of West Coast Christian Writers

"I have never felt so connected to an author while reading a Bible Study. Shadia Hrichi is a refreshingly real and relatable, grace-filled guide who roots this heartbreaking account within its historical context and God's plan of redemption. Witnessing Tamar's transformation from a mistreated, abandoned young widow into a powerful catalyst for change illuminates what God can accomplish through us and in us, even in the midst of our most painful circumstances. For anyone who has ever felt betrayed or deceived, this study is a blessing and a balm."

—**Rosie Makinney,** author, podcaster, and founder of Fight For Love Ministries

"Shadia is an engaging and knowledgeable guide who holds her reader's hand throughout the broader story of Tamar, while still creating room for individuals to listen for God's truth specifically for them. She integrates passages from both the Old and New Testaments, so those looking for an interactive but comprehensive approach to understanding the biblical narrative will be equipped to dive deep into this story of redemption."

—**Andrea Coli,** teaching pastor and Christian speaker

"From the first pages of this in-depth Bible study, Shadia Hrichi reveals her knowledge of Scripture and her desire for us to be transformed by truth. With consideration for the whole counsel of God's Word, Hrichi dives deep into the story of an abandoned woman to show us that God makes the powerless secure and invites the abandoned to belong."

—**Shawna Marie Bryant,** podcaster and author of *Longing to Belong: Discovering the Joy of Acceptance*

BEHIND THE SEEN
Exploring the Bible's Unsung Heroes

TAMAR

Rediscovering the God Who Redeems Me

Shadia Hrichi

LEAFWOOD
PUBLISHERS
an imprint of Abilene Christian University Press

TAMAR

Rediscovering the God Who Redeems Me

an imprint of Abilene Christian University Press

Copyright © 2021 by Shadia Hrichi

ISBN 978-1-68426-301-1

Printed in the United States of America

ALL RIGHTS RESERVED
No part of this publication may be reproduced, stored in a retrieval system, or transmitted in any form by any means—electronic, mechanical, photocopying, recording, or otherwise—without prior written consent.

Scripture quotations, unless otherwise noted, are from The ESV® Bible (The Holy Bible, English Standard Version®) copyright © 2001 by Crossway, a publishing ministry of Good News Publishers. ESV® Text Edition: 2016. All rights reserved.

Scripture quotations marked NIV are taken from The Holy Bible, New International Version®, NIV® copyright © 1973, 1978, 1984, 2011 by Biblica, Inc.® Used by permission. All rights reserved worldwide.

Scripture quotations marked NKJV are taken from the New King James Version® copyright © 1982 by Thomas Nelson. Used by permission. All rights reserved.

Scripture quotations marked NLT are taken from the Holy Bible, New Living Translation, copyright ©1996, 2004, 2007, 2015 by Tyndale House Foundation. Used by permission of Tyndale House Publishers, Inc., Carol Stream, IL 60188. All rights reserved.

Cataloging-in-Publication Data is on file at the Library of Congress, Washington, DC.

Cover design by ThinkPen Design | Interior text design by Strong Design, Sandy Armstrong

Leafwood Publishers is an imprint of Abilene Christian University Press
ACU Box 29138
Abilene, Texas 79699

1-877-816-4455
www.leafwoodpublishers.com

21 22 23 24 25 26 27 / 7 6 5 4 3 2 1

I dedicate this study to my dear friend and ministry partner, Sandi Miller.
Like many others, whose stories few will know this side of heaven,
your life and love for Jesus quietly and courageously display
the beauty and power of God's redemption—and those who know you are
enriched because of it.

But now thus says the L<small>ORD</small> . . .
"Fear not, for I have redeemed you;
I have called you by name, you are mine."

Isaiah 43:1

CONTENTS

Acknowledgments 9
About the Author 11
About the Study 13
Group Study Tips 15
A Note from the Author 17

Part I: Abandoned
Week One: Anticipating God's Fulfillment 21
Week Two: Marveling at God's Forbearance 59
Week Three: Lessons from God's Flood 97

Part II: Abiding
Week Four: Trusting in God's Favor 135
Week Five: Praising God's Faithfulness 173

Part III: Adopted
Week Six: Adopted into God's Family 211
Genealogy of Jesus Christ 247

ACKNOWLEDGMENTS

Scripture teaches that as God's people, we are "one body with many parts." The longer I serve in ministry, the more I realize how true this is. While my name may be on the cover of this study, I did not get here on my own.

There is no greater foundation on which to build a ministry than prayer. Thank you to John and Carolyn Jacobson, Liz Nunez, Sandi Miller, Linda Dunning, Dave and Chris Ryan, Carole Swan, Jeannie Pittam, Anne Brown, Kendra Burrows, Kiki Myabathula, and so many other dear saints I haven't the space to list here who are part of my Ministry Prayer Team. Your faithful prayers over the years are the foundational strength of this ministry.

To Liz Curtis-Higgs, thank you, dear sister, for reading this manuscript and offering such a kind endorsement. Your generous heart to squeeze me into your "calendar that runneth over" is truly a gift (I still chuckle at your words!). And thank you also, Francine Rivers, for introducing us, as well as the added blessing of your endorsement.

To Susy Flory, Rosie Makinney, Andrea Coli, and Shawna Marie Bryant, thank you for reading this study in the midst of managing your own ministry demands and busy schedules. I am truly grateful to each of you for your endorsement of this study and sacrifice of time.

To Jason Fikes, Mary Hardegree, and Duane Anderson of Leafwood Publishers. Jason, I always appreciate your exceptional ability to help take my final draft a couple of notches higher; thank you! Mary, thank you for polishing the manuscript with your superb editing. And Duane, thank you for all you do to take each published work and help launch it into the world! I am also delighted with Greg Jackson of ThinkPen Design for another stellar cover, and to Sandy Armstrong of Strong Design for her stunning interior text design.

To my amazing team of beta readers, Sandi Miller, Linda Dunning, Kendra Burrows, and Karen Mutsch, can I just say, "you rock!" Each one of you brings a unique perspective that has helped to enrich this study in ways I could not have done on my own.

To the precious women in my life group, better known as the "Best Small Group Ever," God could not have blessed me with a more wonderful group of women to share life with. I love you, dear sisters.

Thank you to my church family of Venture Christian, along with so many other family members and friends who have blessed me with your love, prayers, and encouragement over the years in more ways than I can count. I could not do this ministry without you.

Most of all, I give praise to the One without whom I would have nothing of value to share. Thank You, King Jesus, for redeeming my broken life from the pit. For as long as I have breath, I will praise You for all you have done. I am continually humbled that You would entrust me to teach Your holy Word. May the precious truths in this book stir many hearts to love You even more because of the glorious redemption You purchased for us by Your own blood. To Your Name alone be all glory and praise forever!

ABOUT THE AUTHOR

SHADIA HRICHI IS A PASSIONATE BIBLE teacher, author, and speaker who has a heart for seeing lives transformed by the power of God's Word. Having experienced much heartache, including a broken home, abortion, and divorce, Shadia captures the hearts of her audience as she illustrates God's love, faithfulness, and power of redemption through her personal experiences.

She received a master's degree in biblical and theological studies from Western Seminary, as well as a master's degree in criminal justice from the State University of New York. Shadia is the author of several Bible studies, including *Legion* and *Hagar*, both in her Behind the Seen series, and *Worthy of Love*, a story-driven Bible study for post-abortion healing. In addition to teaching Bible studies, Shadia is often invited to speak at churches, conferences, and other events. Her insightful and witty yet vulnerable teaching style reveals compassion for the hurting, love for Jesus, and uncompromising commitment to the truth of God's Word.

Shadia, who resides in Northern California, is an active member of Venture Christian Church and loves visiting the ocean each week for "a date with Jesus." Be sure to visit www.shadiahrichi.com and sign up for updates. *Tamar* is the third study in her series, Behind the Seen: Exploring the Bible's Unsung Heroes. Be among the first to be notified of the next study!

ABOUT THE STUDY

WELCOME, FRIEND! YOU ARE IN FOR AN ADVENTURE. THE story of Tamar, with all its sordid twists and turns, could not be a more fitting place to embark on a journey of *Rediscovering the God Who Redeems Me*.

This book is divided into six weeks, each comprising five days of personal study. For added flexibility, choose a commitment level that works best for you: "light" (15 minutes/day), "moderate" (30 minutes/day), "in-depth" (45 minutes/day), or "all-in" (60 minutes/day). See Group Study Tips (on the next page) for more details.

Each day of study includes one or more questions suitable for group discussion. These questions are followed by a ⌘. Be sure not to overlook these questions, even if you are working through the material on your own. There are also Pause to Ponder sections throughout the study; these are designed to provide you with a time of personal reflection. Use the space in the margin (or, if you prefer, a journal or notebook) to respond to these questions. For readers desiring to dig even deeper, I've prepared Extra questions, which are preceded by a ⌘.

At the end of each day, there is a Your Turn section for personal application. These questions are important. While studying the Bible can stir our hearts and open our eyes to wonderful truths, only when we apply what we have learned will it have a lasting impact for God's kingdom. In addition to this workbook, optional video teaching sessions are available at www.shadiahrichi.com/tamar.

During my study of Tamar, I often found myself fascinated by secondary topics related to the material. The Supplemental Readings I included throughout the study are not essential, but you may find them enjoyable and informative. I have included a section called Group Study Tips, which you may find useful if you are doing the study as a group.

One quick note: some paraphrase versions of the Bible may be inadequate for the purposes of this study. Whenever possible, it is recommended that you complete the exercises using a Bible translation that adheres to a more literal translation, such as the English Standard Version, New American Standard Bible, New King James Version, or King James Version.

Before you begin, take a few moments to ask the Holy Spirit to guide you over the next six weeks and to bless your commitment to this study. Then, as you open your Bible and your heart, begin each day with an eager expectation of *Rediscovering the God Who Redeems Me*.

GROUP STUDY TIPS

BECAUSE ANY DEEP WORK OF GOD REQUIRES A SACRIFICE of time spent in His Word and in His presence, the volume of material in an in-depth study can be challenging for some participants. For this reason, several suggestions are provided to help you facilitate the study when participants have varying levels of time constraints.

Video Teaching Sessions

Seven optional video teaching sessions serve to complement and enhance the study. Watch Session One before you begin. Then, watch Session Two through Session Six before completing Week Two through Week Six in the study. Finally, as a wrap-up, watch Session Seven when you finish the study. Session One is approximately 15 minutes; Sessions Two, Three, Four, Five, Six, and Seven are between 20 and 25 minutes in length. Video sessions are available at www.shadiahrichi.com/tamar.

Plan an Extended Schedule

Instead of meeting for six weeks, allow two weeks for each chapter, for a total of twelve weeks. Every other week, invite participants to watch and discuss Shadia's video teaching sessions. These modifications will also provide periodic opportunities for participants to "catch up" on anything they may have missed or to spend extra time on areas of the study they may wish to explore further.

Customized Commitments for a Six-Week Schedule

Based on a six-week format, the following are suggested assignments based on an individual's time constraints.

For All Participants

- Read through each day's material, including the assigned Bible passages.
- Optional: read the Supplemental Reading section as provided in various weeks.

Light (15 Minutes a Day)

- Complete the Your Turn personal application section at the end of each day.
- If you have time, complete the Group Discussion questions, identified with a ⌇.

Moderate (30 Minutes a Day)

- Complete the various Pause to Ponder personal reflection sections as well as the Your Turn personal application section at the end of each day.
- Complete the Group Discussion questions identified with a ⌇.

In-Depth (45 Minutes a Day)

- Complete all questions except for the Extra questions identified with a ⌇.

All-In (60 Minutes a Day)

- Complete all the questions, including the Extra questions identified with a ⌇.
- Read all the Supplemental Reading sections.

May the Lord bless you as you journey through this study!

A NOTE FROM THE AUTHOR

EVER SINCE I WAS A CHILD, I HAVE LOVED CHEERING FOR the underdogs. Whether I am watching a movie, reading a novel, or hearing of real-life events, my heart is drawn to those who face impossible odds and seem to have everything going against them. Maybe that's one of the reasons why I gravitate toward certain stories in the Bible. It is no accident that I named this series Behind the Seen: Exploring the Bible's Unsung Heroes. Like Hagar and the man with the Legion, Tamar is an example of someone often overlooked, not only during the time when she lived, but in today's preaching and teaching as well.

Though few may take notice of Tamar, God chose to weave her into His grand redemptive story for a reason. Like many unsung heroes, Tamar had a lot going against her, especially in the time and culture in which she lived. Not only was she a woman, she was also a Canaanite—an ethnic group that God's people were strictly forbidden to marry. If those strikes against her were not enough, at one point she even disguised herself as a prostitute and . . . well, we will get to that soon enough.

Simply mentioning Tamar's name to those who have heard of her story can invite all kinds of reactions: a lip curl in disgust, a groan of disdain, perhaps a sigh of pity. Plenty are quick to judge, but few have explored the depths of her story. Like many events in the Bible, if we take the time to dig deep into God's Word, to examine how the story fits into the bigger picture, we will often discover that there is far more going on *behind the seen*. As you explore Tamar's story in the coming weeks, you will have an opportunity to decide for yourself. Some call her courageous; others pronounce condemnation. Nonetheless, within the bounds of God's sovereignty, Tamar's choices altered the trajectory of human history, and they still echo in the heavens today.

When we look back through the generations, even among God's own people, we discover that Tamar was not alone. All of human history is basically an unending cycle of dysfunction and failure, but in His mercy, God does not abandon us there! His plan of redemption was written from eternity past, in spite of the dysfunction, failure, and sin that He knew would unfold along the way. For reasons known only to Him, God chose to invite Tamar into His glorious plan.

So, my friend, are you ready for an adventure? Are you ready for a story of a woman facing impossible odds, whose life intersects with the One who overcomes the impossible? Then come with me! Let's rediscover the *God Who Redeems Me*!

Your sister in Christ,

Shadia

In him we have redemption through his blood,
the forgiveness of our trespasses,
according to the riches of his grace.

Ephesians 1:7

PART I

ABANDONED

NOTES

ANTICIPATING FULFILLMENT

WEEK ONE

From the beginning, God has been setting apart a people to call His own—a people to reflect His image in the world. This week, we will trace how God has been at work *behind the seen* throughout the generations of man, setting apart a people for Himself, from Adam to Seth to Noah, to Abraham, Isaac, and Jacob. As we journey through their stories, we will encounter triumph and tragedy, life and death, joy and sorrow.

When we come to the story of Jacob's wife, Leah, the trajectory of God's people takes a sudden turn, paving the way for Tamar's entrance into His grand redemptive story.

Day One
Being Set Apart by God

*The book of the genealogy of Jesus Christ, the son of David,
the son of Abraham. Abraham was the father of Isaac,
and Isaac the father of Jacob, and Jacob the father of Judah and
his brothers, and Judah the father of Perez and Zerah by Tamar.*

Matthew 1:1–3

Fun fact: Tamar's name is pronounced *Tah-mahr* in Hebrew, with the emphasis on the second syllable.

Three verses. Tamar's name appears just three verses into the New Testament, but her story doesn't begin there. Like all of our stories, hers begins at the beginning, the first chapters in the book of Genesis. Just as we wouldn't want to begin reading a novel midway through the book, before we can dive into Tamar's story, we will first spend a few days taking in the big picture in which her story appears.

Hero Stories

Genesis is a fascinating book to study because it is by and large a historical narrative. But it is more than that. I love how the *ESV Study Bible* describes it: "the book of Genesis is primarily a collection of what may be called hero stories...."[1]

Hero stories. I like that!

The other night, I watched the animated movie *The Incredibles*. When I was growing up, I loved watching the television programs *The Six Million Dollar Man* and *The Bionic Woman*—action-packed stories of ordinary people given superhuman strength to carry out high-risk missions for the good of humanity. Who doesn't love a good hero story?

> ### PAUSE TO PONDER
> Name someone whom you consider or have considered to be a hero, now or when you were a child. The person can be real or fictional, in or outside the Bible. What makes this person heroic?

Record your thoughts in the margin; do this for all Pause to Ponder sections.

To this day, there is no shortage of hero stories, both real and imagined. We find them in books and on television, in the movies and on the news. Our hearts are naturally drawn to hero stories. Why? The simple answer is that we need heroes. We need them because we live in a broken world. Everywhere we look, we find injustice and tragedy—things that, in the depths of our soul, remind us that this is not how the world should be. So we gravitate toward hero stories—stories of hope, of triumph, of good conquering evil. If we lived in a world where no one needed saving, there would be no need for heroes.

When we think about heroes in the Bible—such as Moses standing up to Pharaoh or David conquering Goliath—we can't help but celebrate their victories. The Bible is filled with stories of heroes: Noah, Abraham, Esther, Samson, and so many others. But all too often we forget that the same Moses who stood up to Pharaoh also murdered a man and buried him in the sand. The same David

Day One / Week One

who killed Goliath also killed his faithful servant, Uriah. Even the great King Solomon, blessed by God with surpassing wisdom, eventually succumbed to—of all things—idolatry.

When it comes to the human race, sooner or later, even the best heroes will fall short. No matter how strong, wise, wealthy, or successful, no one can escape the ravages of sin—the underlying first cause of all evil, sorrow, and suffering in our world.[2] The truth of the matter is that when it comes to saving the human race from sin, we need more than a hero; we need a Savior. And three chapters into the book of Genesis, God, in His mercy, promises one.

Write Genesis 3:15 below. (Optional: read all of Genesis 3:1-15.)

> When it comes to the human race, even the best heroes will fall short. In truth, we need more than a hero; we need a Savior.

Set Apart by God

As soon as sin enters the world, God distinguishes the offspring (or seed) of the serpent and the offspring of the woman. Because the human race has fallen into sin, God pronounces the inevitable: a future of conflict and hostility, pain and sorrow . . . but in the end, triumph! Humanity needs rescue, and praise God that through the offspring of the woman, a Savior will one day come.

Read Genesis 4:1-8. Briefly describe the events.

Why did the Lord look favorably on one offering over the other? What distinguishing factor is emphasized in the text? (Hint: see Proverbs 3:9.)

PAUSE TO PONDER

Consider the effect of sin in just one generation. Do you find it surprising? Not so surprising? Disheartening? Share your thoughts.

One generation. One! One generation into human history, and the first person born to the first human couple murders his own brother in cold blood. If Genesis is a collection of hero stories, we don't seem to be off to a good start. Let's look at the passage more closely, beginning with verses 1–2a, which reads: "Now Adam knew Eve his wife, and she conceived and bore Cain, saying, 'I have gotten a man with the help of the Lord.' And again, she bore his brother Abel."

Because the passage mentions only one conception immediately followed by two births, commentary author John Calvin proposes that Cain and Abel may have been twins, an idea passed on from earlier Jewish rabbis and teachers.[3] It is a reasonable possibility, not only based on the construction of the text ("And again, she bore" can also read, "Then she bore again" as translated in the New King James Version), but also in light of God's blessing on Adam and Eve to be "fruitful and multiply" (Gen. 1:28). In the Bible, we are certain of at least two sets of twins (we will cover these in the weeks ahead), each of which holds a prominent place in the genealogy of God's people. Whether or not Cain and Abel were twins, their violent clash would set a tragic trajectory for generations to come.

The Evil and the Righteous

In the account of Cain and Abel, we read that each brother brought an offering to the Lord out of his labor. Though both engaged in noble pursuits (agriculture and shepherding), it was the quality of their gifts that exposed the degree of reverence in their hearts.

> Look back at Genesis 4:3-7. In the table below, list the only two types of behavior the Lord describes and their respective outcomes, according to verses 6-7. I filled in one box for you.

Behavior	Outcome
Do well	

> Ponder the above table. What conclusions can you draw?

"The heart is deceitful above all things, and desperately sick; who can understand it?"
—Jeremiah 17:9

Day One / Week One

Read Genesis 4:8-9. What does the Lord ask Cain? How does Cain respond?

Since the Lord knows everything, why do you think He asked Cain this question? What does it reveal about the Lord's character?

How about Cain? What does his response reveal about his character?

Already we see the Lord's mercy at work. Cain just murdered his own brother, yet the Lord does not begin the conversation with an accusation, but a question. Just as He did for Adam (Gen. 3:9), the Lord, in His grace, provides Cain an opportunity to confess his sin. Sadly, Cain not only refuses to confess, but he boldly lies to the Lord's face! In fact, he questions the Lord in return! No pity. No remorse. Just defiance. This from the first person born to the human race. Oh, how this must have grieved God's heart!

What reason(s) may have been behind Cain's actions?

Read 1 John 3:12. Fill in the blanks based on the text.

> We should not be like Cain, who was of the _____ one and murdered his _____. And why did he murder him? Because his own deeds were _____ and his brother's _____.

"Precious in the sight of the LORD is the death of his saints." —Psalm 116:15

Though the Lord warned Cain, urging him to "do well" (Gen. 4:7), Cain's behavior only became worse, revealing the cold heart within. Scripture describes Cain as being "of the evil one." That's quite a pronouncement.

In contrast, how does Scripture describe Abel, according to Hebrews 11:4?

Anticipating God's Fulfillment

Right from the start, we see a clear distinction between Cain and Abel, and we see the "evil one" already at work in the interaction between these first children of man with "the seed of the serpent striking quickly at the seed of the woman in an attempt to prevent the fulfillment of the prophecy of Genesis 3:15."[4]

Who Is My Brother?

Read Genesis 4:10-11. Write the Lord's response to Cain, according to verse 10.

What does the Lord's response reveal about His heart?

> "By this it is evident who are the children of God, and who are the children of the devil: whoever does not practice righteousness is not of God, nor is the one who does not love his brother." —1 John 3:10

Examine Genesis 4:1-11 in your Bible. Mark (highlight, circle, or underline) each occurrence of the word *brother*. How many times is this word used to describe Abel? How many times is it used to describe Cain?

Abel _____ times   Cain _____ times

- Do you think this is significant? Why or why not?

In the New Testament, believers are repeatedly and affectionately called "brothers" (often referring to both male and female siblings within God's family). In Genesis, it is no coincidence that only Abel is described as a "brother"—not once, but seven times! In the Bible, the number seven is symbolic for completion or fullness. Scripture is revealing that Abel is a "brother" in the fullest sense of the word.

.... YOUR TURN ....

But you are a chosen race, a royal priesthood, a holy nation, a people for his own possession, that you may proclaim the excellencies of him who called you out of darkness into his marvelous light.

1 Peter 2:9

What difference does it make that God sets apart a people for Himself? For example:

Day One / Week One

- What difference has it made in your life?

- How about in your family or church?

- What about the world? What difference does it make in the world today that there is a group of people whom God has set apart for Himself?

Day Two
Calling on the Name of the Lord

Yesterday, we saw how beautifully Scripture brought Abel's heart to light by describing him as a brother—not once, but seven times. In contrast, Cain is never once described that way; he exhibits no brotherly affection, concern, or love. On the surface, he may have seemed entirely amicable until jealousy and sin exposed the cold, empty heart within.

Good Fruit vs. Bad Fruit

My favorite evening snack is a bowl of popcorn and a plate of orange slices or a tall glass of orange juice (with lots of pulp). I love oranges. I still remember the first time I was living away from home and went grocery shopping for myself. When I came to the produce section, I happily filled a plastic bag with a half dozen large, bright oranges. I couldn't wait to get home and try one (with a bowl of popcorn, of course!). Later that evening, I took a knife and eagerly cut into one of the oranges. The orange was vibrant and firm on the outside, but when I sliced into the skin, it was nearly an inch thick! Not only that, but when I finally reached the fruit inside, it was a fraction of the size I expected and nearly half shriveled. What a disappointment!

Looks can be deceiving. What appeared sweet and delicious on the outside turned out to be dry and shriveled on the inside. Only later did I learn the trick of weighing the fruit in my hand to assess how much plump fruit and heavy juice lay hidden within. In the same way, God knows every corner of our hearts. Nothing is hidden from His sight.

> "Every way of a man is right in his own eyes, but the Lord weighs the heart."
> —Proverbs 21:2

Anticipating God's Fulfillment

Read at least two of the following New Testament passages. What is being contrasted in John 3:6, Romans 8:5-9, Romans 8:13-14, and Galatians 5:16-17?

> ## PAUSE TO PONDER
>
> Think of a time during the past month when you experienced a struggle between flesh and the spirit in your own life. What was the outcome? What did you learn? What would you do differently next time?

The Fallout from Sin

Read Genesis 4:10-16 (verses 10 and 11 are a review). Below are various consequences of Cain's actions. Using the keywords, fill in the blanks based on the text.

strength   presence   cursed   wanderer   mark

Cain is _____ from the ground.

The ground will no longer yield its _____.

Cain will be a fugitive and a _____ on the earth.

The Lord put a _____ on Cain.

Then Cain went away from the _____ of the Lord.

Compare Genesis 4:14 with Genesis 3:8. What principle(s) are at work in these passages?

After the Lord's confrontation with Cain, He pronounces judgment: Cain is cursed from the ground and will become a wanderer on the earth. When Cain expresses fear that someone will find and kill him, the Lord declares, "Not so! If anyone kills Cain, vengeance shall be taken on him sevenfold" (Gen. 4:15). As mentioned yesterday, the number seven represents completion or fullness. This means whoever kills Cain will likewise be paid back in full; that is, he would forfeit his own life. The Lord then places a mark on Cain to serve as a warning against would-be attackers (Deut. 32:35).

Scholars have been debating the nature of this "mark" for two millennia. Was it a physical mark? An ailment? The speculations are endless; therefore, we must be exceedingly cautious in any attempt to define its appearance or nature. One commentator writes that the expression "does not appear to indicate something 'on' Cain as much as something 'for' him. . . . Most important, it is a mark of *protection* . . . not infamy and degradation."[5] In short, the text makes no attempt to describe the mark (therefore, neither should we); rather, the emphasis is on its purpose. The mark assures Cain that the Lord, in His mercy, will not require Cain's life at this time—a perfect depiction of both God's law and grace.

Read Romans 2:4. How does this verse shed light on God's actions toward Cain?

Read Genesis 4:17-19 and 4:23-24. List everything the text reveals about Lamech. What do these details suggest about Lamech's character? (Hint: see Gen. 2:24 and 4:10.)

Read Genesis 4:17-19. In the space below, fill in the names of the generations descended from Adam through his son Cain. I completed a few of them for you.

Adam

Cain

_____

_____

Mehujael

Methushael

_____

Anticipating God's Fulfillment

How many generations are represented from Adam through Cain until the writer pauses the genealogy to tell us about the next person whose behavior goes completely against God's design and will? What significance may this number have? (Hint: consider the character and behavior of the person in the seventh generation.)

Polygamy. Murder. Even boasting about them! Lamech, the seventh generation from Adam through Cain, is the culmination of the evil line of Cain. In the span of seven generations, God's design for marriage, "[the two] shall become one flesh" (Gen. 2:24; Mark 10:8), is violated. Further, Lamech murders a man for simply striking him. And if these were not enough, he then announces that should anyone retaliate, vengeance would be seventy-seven times. In other words, Lamech will even outdo God's decree! But none of this should be surprising.

Look once again at Genesis 4:17-24. How many times is the Lord referenced in the passage? What conclusions can you draw?

> "Your iniquities have made a separation between you and your God, and your sins have hidden his face from you so that he does not hear." —Isaiah 59:2

The words, "Then Cain went away from the presence of the LORD" (Gen. 4:16), convey far more than physical proximity. Despite the Lord's mercy and opportunities to choose differently, Cain's cold heart only grew worse. Sadly, his descendants followed in his footsteps.

But there is hope.

Read Genesis 4:25-26. What happens after the birth of Seth's firstborn son?

Contrast the lineage of Cain with the brief introduction to the lineage of Seth. What observations can you make?

Day Two / Week One

A Glimmer of Hope

I did not grow up going to church or believing in God. I was thirty years old before I heard the good news that Jesus died for my sins and was raised to life, offering the hope of salvation to all who follow Him. Six months later, God, in His grace, opened my eyes to His love. I asked Jesus to forgive my sins and be the Lord of my life. That was more than twenty years ago, and to this day, I continue hoping and praying that my loved ones will likewise embrace the glorious gift of God's love and salvation through Jesus Christ. This is God's desire as well. It has been God's desire for every human soul since the beginning.

After the disaster between Cain and Abel, followed by the continued degeneration of Cain's family line, a glimmer of hope arrives.

> On the chart on page 247, cross out the name of Adam's firstborn, Cain, and write the name Seth above "Adam."

At the end of Genesis 4, we are introduced to Seth's family line, at which point the name of the Lord reenters the story. But there may be something else implied by the last verse (Gen. 4:26). Most English translations add the words *people* (or *men*) and *upon* (or *on*) to bring clarification: "At that time people began to call upon the name of the LORD." However, in the original Hebrew, the subject is not stated. The Hebrew verb translated as *began* is passive, not active, suggesting that the action "to call" is happening to the unnamed subject(s). Another commentator presents a view shared by a number of early scholars, which is that Genesis 4:26 informs us that the family line of Seth is "now being called by the name Yahweh [the Lord]—that is, they are the *sons of God* . . ."⁶ (emphasis mine).

When we consider what we have discovered so far in the early chapters of Genesis, the notion that Seth's family line is being called by the name of the Lord fits perfectly into the unfolding of the entire narrative to this point, which is that God is setting apart a godly line of people to call His own.

> Read Genesis 5:1-5. Who is left out at the start of Adam's genealogy? What reason(s) might the author have had for doing so? (Hint: compare Genesis 1:27 with Genesis 5:3.)

Anticipating God's Fulfillment

Read Genesis 5:6-24. In the space below, fill in the names of the generations descending from Adam through his son Seth. I completed a few of them for you.

Adam

Seth

_____

Kenan

_____

_____

_____

How many generations are represented from Adam through Seth until the author pauses the genealogy to tell us about the first person described as one who "walked with God" (Gen. 5:22)? What significance may this number have? (Hint: consider what Scripture records about the person in the seventh generation.)

Try to imagine living in these earliest generations of human history. Apart from Genesis 3:15, little is known about God's redemptive plan for the world. Nevertheless, how does Genesis 5:24 offer hope?

Read Hebrews 11:5, and complete the sentence: "By _____ Enoch was taken up so that he should not see _____."

How are faith and death connected in the above passage?

Day Two / Week One

Read John 8:51 in the margin. How could Jesus make such a claim? (Hint: see Matthew 20:28 and John 3:36 and 5:24.)

"Truly, truly, I say to you, if anyone keeps my word, he will never see death."
—John 8:51

PAUSE TO PONDER

To walk with God does not mean to live a life of sinless perfection but instead one characterized by faithful devotion and a sincere desire to obey God. How would you rate your walk with God right now? Place an X on the line.

not walking with God ———————————— perfect commitment

What difference has walking with God made in your life? If you are not currently walking with God or have never committed your life to Christ, what may be holding you back?

The mention of Enoch is brief, but its message could not be more profound. Enoch, the seventh generation from Adam through Seth, is the culmination of the godly line of Seth, of those who "call upon the name of the Lord" (Gen. 4:26). His life gives us a glimpse into the hope of eternal life for all who walk with God and live by faith.

In seven generations . . .

- The line of Adam through Cain reaches its full measure of sin and wickedness.
- The line of Adam through Seth offers a glimpse at the hope of eternal life.
- Two family lines descended from Adam, each headed in a different direction . . . or are they?

Read Genesis 5:28–29.

Here again, we are reminded of sin's curse, and the fact that no one is immune from its consequences. At this point in the story, there are two distinct groups of people living together on the earth: the degenerate line of Cain and the godly line

Anticipating God's Fulfillment

of Seth—and their worlds are about to clash. But before that happens, a glimmer of hope is seen on the horizon. Another hero is about to enter the story. By God's grace, he arrives just in time.

YOUR TURN

We have certainly done some digging into the first families of the book of Genesis. Their stories provide an important backdrop to understanding God's activity in the world, particularly in the generations leading up to Tamar's entrance into the story. While the generations of Cain spiraled further into sin and away from God's presence, we reached a critical turning point with the line of Seth when the name of the Lord reentered the story.

> How about your family? Who was the first person to "call on the name of the Lord" in your family? (It may even be you!) What difference has it made in your life and in the lives of other family members?

> Write a prayer of gratitude for God's presence in your life and in your family.

> If no one in your family, perhaps including yourself, has yet become a Christian, what may be standing in the way? Bring your sincere questions and struggles to God in prayer. He loves you and delights in honest conversation.

Day Two / Week One

DAY THREE
Taking Comfort in Second Chances

When I was six years old, my parents invited a gathering of friends and neighbors to our home for a New Year's Eve party. To keep me occupied, Mom and Dad assigned me tasks to help with the party. At one point, my dad brought me into our kitchen where he had placed a dozen glasses on the dining table. Next to the glasses were two bottles of soda: one of Coke and one of 7-Up. He then instructed me to fill the glasses, half with Coke and half with 7-Up. When finished, I was to bring the glasses one at a time into the living room and serve the guests. I was delighted to be given such an important assignment. As soon as my father left, I promptly got to work.

I opened the bottle of Coke. Pouring the dark bubbly soda into each glass, I did my best to fill each glass precisely halfway, just as my father had instructed. Then I opened the 7-Up and proceeded to fill each glass to the top. When I brought the drinks into the living room and began serving the guests, I noticed some odd expressions on the guests' faces as they took their first sips. It didn't take long for my father to realize my mistake. The entire round of refreshments was ruined. My father shook his head and released me from my duties. Who knew a six-year-old could be so literal!

A Bad Mix

Yesterday, we traced seven generations of the two family lines descended from Adam: one through Cain and the other through Seth. A glimmer of hope arrives in the line of Seth when Noah is born. Whether or not you have read Noah's story, chances are you have heard of his name and the worldwide flood that marked his life. Today, we will take a brief look at the events that prompted the flood. These events will provide surprising insights when Tamar enters the story, so we don't want to miss it!

Although we see the distinctions between the family lines of Cain and Seth, when Adam and Eve sinned in their garden paradise so long ago, the entire human race became polluted with sin (Rom. 5:12). Not only that, but it would be only a matter of time before the family lines of Seth and Cain would mix through intermarriage. But there is hope. Scripture tells us that just before God pronounced judgment, "Noah found favor in the eyes of the Lord" (Gen. 6:8).

Read Genesis 6:1–8.

> "The Lord looks down from heaven on the children of man, to see if there are any who understand, who seek after God. They have all turned aside; together they have become corrupt; there is none who does good, not even one."
> —Psalm 14:2-3

What is the first thing we are told that went wrong?

Who provoked God, according to verses 3 and 5?

Compare Genesis 6:1-2 with Genesis 4:16-19. What similarities do you notice?

"For all who are led by the Spirit of God are sons of God." —Romans 8:14

SUPPLEMENTAL READING

Who Are the "sons of God"?

The identity of the "sons of God" in Genesis 6:2 and 6:4 is debated among scholars. This is the perfect place to pause and conduct a brief word study.

The following table lists the use of "son(s) of God" (or equivalent) in other Old Testament[7] passages. (In the New Testament, "sons of God" always refers to believers.[8]) Read the Scripture references, and complete the table by filling in the remaining boxes.

References	How is the subject described?	Who is being referred to?
Exodus 4:22	firstborn son (of the Lord)	Israel
Deuteronomy 14:1		Israelites
2 Samuel 7:14	son (of God the Father)	King Solomon
Psalm 82:6	sons of the Most High	Israel's leaders/judges
Hosea 1:10		Israelites
Isaiah 1:2, 43:6	children of God; sons and daughters of the Lord	
Job 1:6, 2:1,[9] and 38:7	sons of God	angelic beings (not fallen)

Day Three / Week One

In the Old Testament, in addition to the two occurrences in Genesis 6, the expression "sons of God" (or equivalent) appears in a variety of passages. Among these, only in the book of Job does the term "sons of God" seem to describe angelic beings[10]—specifically, angels that have not fallen into sin. In both Job 1:6 and 2:1, the author (who is unknown) writes, "There was a day when the sons of God came to present themselves before the LORD, and Satan also came among them." In both verses, Satan is distinguished separately from "sons of God." He goes *among* them, but he is not identified *with* them.

To further help us discern whether "sons of God" in Genesis 6 might refer to angelic beings, an important rule of biblical interpretation is to consider how language is used elsewhere in the same book. For example, in the book of Genesis, when the author wants to describe angels, he simply writes "angels of God" (see Gen. 28:12 and 32:1). Additional references to "angel of the LORD" or "angel of God" also appear throughout Genesis. For the author to use different terminology, namely "sons of God," to refer to angels in Genesis 6 would be inconsistent with his writing elsewhere in the book.

Read Genesis 6:12-13. On whom does God lay blame for the corruption and violence on the earth? (See also Gen. 8:21.) How does this help inform who the "sons of God" might be in Genesis 6?

When trying to understand difficult passages, it is helpful to step back and refresh our memory as to what information was provided in previous passages to provide context. Let's do that now.

In Genesis 6:8, we read that "Noah found favor in the eyes of the LORD." What family line did Noah descend from? Circle one.

        line of Cain   line of Seth

On the chart on page 247, above "Seth," write the name Noah.

What role may Noah's ancestry have in the story? (Hint: glance back at Genesis 4:26.)

Anticipating God's Fulfillment

> "You shall not intermarry with them, giving your daughters to their sons or taking their daughters for your sons."; "For [the people of Israel] have taken some of their daughters to be wives ... so that the holy race has mixed itself with the peoples of the lands."
>
> —Deuteronomy 7:3; Ezra 9:2

Now, let's go back and take a closer look at what prompted this disastrous judgment in the first place.

Reread Genesis 6:2. List two or three possibilities as to who the "sons of God" might be.

Skip ahead to the New Testament and read Luke 3:38. How is Adam described in the genealogy? How does this help inform who the "sons of God" might be in Genesis 6?

While some biblical commentators hold that the "sons of God" in Genesis 6 refers to angels, others are persuaded that they represent the godly line of Seth.[11] This interpretation fits perfectly into the Genesis narrative to this point: the descendants of Seth eventually fell into the pattern of Cain's descendant Lamech by lusting after "the daughters of man" and taking "as their wives any they chose."[12]

Some of the confusion surrounding the passage stems from the mention of the "Nephilim" (simply meaning "giants") in verse 4. Who are they? No one knows for certain, and therefore we need to be extremely careful how much weight we place on this verse as we study the surrounding passage. Nevertheless, there are some things Scripture does tell us.

In Numbers 13:32–33, the Nephilim are described as people "of great height" and "sons of Anak" (who are likewise tall; see Deut. 2:10, 21). Further, in Deuteronomy 9:2, the "sons of Anak" are called "people"—the same Hebrew word (*am*) used to describe the people of Israel a few verses later (Deut. 9:6). Since the Nephilim are referred to both before and after the flood, it would seem that the post-flood "giants" were simply described this way because they resembled the "giants" who lived prior to the flood.[13] If these were simply exceptionally tall men, it makes sense that they existed before and after the flood since they would have descended from Adam (and later, through Noah).

Whatever interpretation one holds, the critical point of the passage lies in the arrival of another hero in the story. Though judgment is coming, one man "found favor in the eyes of the L ORD" (Gen. 6:8).

> Bible study tip: Be careful not to place weight on obscure or highly debated passages to construct your interpretation of a particular text or to formulate your theology (what you believe to be true about God).

Day Three / Week One

PAUSE TO PONDER

Consider Genesis 6:5-6 in the margin. Where would you place an X on the line below in regard to the "wickedness of man" on the earth in Noah's day?

low _____ high

Where would you place an X on the line below in regard to the "wickedness of man" on the earth in our day?

low _____ high

Are your responses the same or different? Why? Share your thoughts.

> "The LORD saw that the wickedness of man was great in the earth, and that every intention of the thoughts of his heart was only evil continually. And the LORD regretted that he had made man on the earth, and it grieved him to his heart."
>
> —Genesis 6:5-6

What Should Have Been

God is all-wise and all-knowing; therefore, He cannot make mistakes. Nevertheless, God's heart breaks over His beloved creatures' rejection of His loving plan and purpose for their lives, which has led to so much sin and suffering in the world. It is the tragic forfeit of what could have been that breaks God's heart. It's the garden of Eden all over again.

After God saves Noah and his family from the worldwide flood, God blesses Noah and his sons, saying, "Be fruitful and multiply and fill the earth" (Gen. 9:1). But as time goes on, we are given a glimpse into the hearts of Noah's sons—not all are good.

> Read Genesis 9:20-27. Compare and contrast Noah's response regarding Shem and Canaan; then, answer the questions that follow. (Note: Canaan was Ham's son; see the endnote regarding the term "curse of Ham.")[14]

Why is Canaan cursed?

Anticipating God's Fulfillment

How is Shem distinguished from the others, according to verse 26?

Do you think the above distinctions are significant? Why or why not?

Interesting Fact: The modern term *Semite* derives from the people descended from Noah's son Shem, who is the ancestor of Israel (along with several other groups). The name Shem means *name*.

How does Noah's response in verses 25-27 compare with God's actions throughout the generations in Genesis we have studied so far?

From our cultural mindset, Noah's responses may seem harsh, but they continue the theme we have seen from the beginning: God is setting apart a godly line for Himself. There is a reason Shem is specifically described as one whose God is the Lord (Gen. 9:26). After Noah's pronouncement on his sons and their descendants, Genesis 10 begins the genealogy of Noah's three sons. However, when we reach the descendants of Shem, the genealogy divides into two.

............................YOUR TURN............................

Our great God and Savior Jesus Christ,
who gave himself for us to redeem us from all lawlessness and
to purify for himself a people for his own possession.

Titus 2:13–14

If the human race continually rejects God's will, why do you suppose God does not wipe people off the face of the earth once and for all? What purpose(s) might God have for repeatedly setting apart a people for Himself?

Day Three / Week One

DAY FOUR
Setting Your Mind on the Things of the Spirit

At the start of this week's lesson, I shared how God has been working *behind the seen* throughout the generations of man, seeking to set apart a people for Himself. In days 1–3, we traced the generations from Adam to Seth to Noah. Today, we will continue tracing God's hand in human history through the stories of Abraham, Isaac, and Jacob. That's a lot of ground to cover, but since this is the family that Tamar will marry into, it provides key context for her story, as we will soon discover.

A New Beginning

We finished yesterday's lesson at a crossroads where the genealogy of Noah's son Shem divides into two.

> Read Genesis 10:21, 25.

Peleg's name means *division*. It is at this point that the genealogy of Shem splits and is traced through Joktan, until we reach Genesis 11.

> Read Genesis 11:1-9. Compare and contrast the people's aim in verse 4 with God's desire for them in Genesis 9:1 and 9:7. How are these in conflict?

So far, we have seen a division between Cain and Abel, then between Cain and Seth, then between Seth's descendent Noah and the rest of the world's population, and then between Noah's son Shem and his brothers. Then we come to yet another divide. Curiously, it is also at this point where we read that "the children of man" had become "one people" (Gen. 11:5–6), but rather than being united in lifting up the name of the Lord, they set out to make a name for themselves. Instead of fulfilling God's desire to multiply and fill the earth, the people instead sought to gather together and "build ourselves a city and a tower with its top in the heavens, and let us make a name for ourselves, lest we be dispersed over the face of the whole earth" (Gen. 11:4)—rejecting the purpose God had for them.

After God steps in and frustrates the people's efforts in building the Tower of Babel (Gen. 11:1–9), Moses returns his attention to the genealogy of Shem. Only this time, rather than tracing it through Joktan, he traces it through Joktan's brother Peleg until we arrive at the Bible's next hero—Abraham.[15]

Anticipating God's Fulfillment

On the chart on page 247, above "Noah," write the name Abraham.

Optional: to trace the genealogy from Shem to Abram/Abraham, read Genesis 11:10-26.

Read Genesis 12:1-3. What does the Lord ask Abraham to leave behind?

Imagine that you are Abraham. Would you feel that God was asking too much? Explain.

Read Joshua 24:2. How is Abraham's father, Terah, described?

What role may Abraham's family background have had in God calling Abraham to leave everything behind?

From Adam to Seth, to Noah, to Abraham, God does not give up easily. He made a promise in that garden paradise long ago, and He will not go back on His word.

PAUSE TO PONDER

> What difference would it make for God to abandon His creation and allow evil to have the final victory in the world? What difference would it make to *you*?

Reflect on Genesis 12:3 in the margin. Does God place any conditions on Abraham in order for God to fulfill His promise to him?

> "I will bless those who bless you, and him who dishonors you I will curse, and in you all the families of the earth shall be blessed." —Genesis 12:3

◦ What difference does this make?

For Christians, Abraham is considered our father of the faith (Rom. 4:11–12). His life and walk with God serve as an example to follow (Gen. 26:5). Nevertheless, like the rest of us, he was a human being born in sin. If you were to dive into the details of Abraham's story, you would encounter a few disappointments along the way. At one point, instead of trusting in God's plan and timing to bless him and Sarah with a son, he allowed his barren wife to talk him into using her Egyptian servant Hagar to produce a child.[16] If using a servant girl to produce a child were not enough, when Abraham feared for his life upon entering new territory, he was willing to put his own wife at risk—not once, but twice![17]

Although God promised Abraham, "in you all the families of the earth shall be blessed" (Gen. 12:3), Abraham's misguided choices would set in motion yet another pattern of family dysfunction that would continue for generations.

PAUSE TO PONDER

Consider a time when you witnessed family dysfunction pass down through the generations (either in your own family or someone you know). How have you seen God at work in breaking destructive cycles? How might God be calling you to intercede for your family, a loved one's family, or even the next generation?

> "These all died in faith, not having received the things promised, but having seen them and greeted them from afar..." —Hebrews 11:13

Abraham eventually "died in faith" (Heb. 11:13), after which God's covenant blessing was passed to Abraham's second son, Isaac.[18]

On the chart on page 247, cross out the name of the firstborn, Ishmael, and write the name Isaac above "Abraham."

Anticipating God's Fulfillment

In time, Isaac's wife Rebekah becomes pregnant with twins. Scripture records that the children "struggled together within her" (Gen. 25:22), prompting Rebekah to seek the Lord about what was happening.

Read Genesis 25:22-28. What is the Lord's response to Rebekah?

What parallels do you notice between Genesis 10:25 and 25:23?

Here we are told of yet another division. Not only are the events surrounding the birth of Isaac's twin sons remarkable (picture the one grabbing his brother's heel!), but they foreshadow a rivalry to come. In this case, the Lord speaks plainly; the older brother will serve the younger. The brothers' future rivalry would be unwittingly reinforced by their own parents—Isaac and Rebekah each had a favorite son.

PAUSE TO PONDER

> Describe a time growing up when you envied the attention given to someone else, perhaps a sibling, a "teachers' pet," or your best friend's *other* friend. Or perhaps you were the one enjoying special treatment. Either way, what challenges did you face? What positive outcomes did you gain from your experience?

Rank Has Its Privileges

In biblical times, birth order was highly significant; it still is in some countries. The firstborn son enjoyed certain privileges. In addition to inheriting a "double portion" of his family's land and possessions after his father's death (Deut. 21:17), the firstborn would also typically assume leadership of the family.

Read Genesis 25:29-34. Briefly summarize the events.

What two or three words would you use to describe Jacob's character in this passage?

Now list two or three words that describe Esau's character.

How does the author sum up the events? Rewrite the last sentence of the passage.

How would you have summed up these events? What stands out most to you?

The Price of a Meal

I am the first to admit it: I can't cook. I basically live on store-bought soups and salads and periodic meals prepared by loving friends who probably worry I would starve otherwise. Still, every once in a while, I'll fire up the stove (mostly to make sure it still works) and make a pot of chili. It's hard to mess up chili. No matter how it comes out, I can always convince myself that I planned it that way. And so, to be honest, I can't imagine anyone bargaining with me for a bowl of anything.

On the other hand, living today in a culture where the benefits of being firstborn mean little more than being spared your siblings' hand-me-downs, it is difficult for most of us to step into the mindset of Jacob. I don't know about you, but when I read about Jacob's behavior, I can't help but shake my head. He thinks nothing of exploiting his brother in his moment of weakness. Demanding Esau's inheritance, Jacob refuses to hand over the bowl of stew unless Esau swears to sell his birthright. "Swear to me now," Jacob orders (Gen. 25:33). Wow. Apart from the fruit that Adam ate in the garden, perhaps no other meal has ever been more costly.[19]

> "For those who live according to the flesh set their minds on the things of the flesh, but those who live according to the Spirit set their minds on the things of the Spirit." —Romans 8:5

Read Hebrews 12:16. How would you define the word *unholy*? What does being unholy look like?

After reading the account in Genesis 25:29-34, would you have described Esau's actions as unholy? Why or why not?

Why might God consider Esau's actions unholy? What do Esau's actions reveal? (Hint: read Romans 8:5 in the margin.)

How can a person "set their mind on the things of the Spirit?" What does that look like?

While Jacob unfairly bargained with Esau, it is Esau's actions that receive the greater condemnation. Commentary author William MacDonald writes, "God does not condone Jacob's wheeling and dealing, but one thing is apparent—Jacob valued the **birthright** and a place in the godly line, while Esau preferred the gratification of his physical appetite to spiritual blessings."[20] Esau would have been well aware of God's promise to his grandfather, Abraham, to make him into a great nation and that, through him, "all the families of the earth shall be blessed" (Gen. 12:3). Whether or not Esau recognized the far-reaching implications of those promises, his impulsive choices and disregard for his birthright had eternal ramifications. Esau not only surrendered his special privileges of receiving a double portion and position of family leader, but he forfeited the honor of being placed in the godly line of the Messiah!

Day Four / Week One

YOUR TURN

Think of a time when you made a hasty decision that cost you more than you bargained for. What did you gain, and what did you lose?

What would you do differently if you could go back?

What can you do now to guard yourself in times when you are tempted to make a hasty, but costly, decision?

> "Enthusiasm without knowledge is no good; haste makes mistakes."
> —Proverbs 19:2 NLT

DAY FIVE
Choosing Praise in the Midst of Sorrow

If you have ever flown on a commercial airplane, then you know that cruising thirty-five thousand feet above the earth at more than five hundred miles per hour can feel like you're hardly moving. However, when the plane finally begins its descent, the closer it gets to landing, the faster it feels, even though the plane is slowing down.

It may not seem like it, but we have been slowing down rapidly. Our exploration into the events from Adam to the flood covered roughly 1,650 years. From the flood to God's call to Abraham was 367 years, and the lives of Abraham, Isaac, and Jacob up to this point cover roughly 125 years. That's more than 2,100 years of history! Perhaps you are wondering why we need such a broad overview. Like you, I am eager to dive into Tamar's story (we're almost there, I promise!), but unless we take the time to see the events of her life in the proper context, we will miss the whole point of it because her story is wrapped up in God's story, and God's story is *big*.

We have two last stops before Tamar's entrance into the narrative. Perhaps you are familiar with the story of Leah, or maybe you are reading her name for the first time. Leah is one of two sisters married to the same man: Jacob. As if that were not bad enough, Jacob isn't interested in Leah at all; rather, he is in love

> Interesting fact: The name Esau may be a wordplay on the Hebrew word *se-ar*, meaning *hair*. Curiously, this is also the Hebrew root word for *goat*, or literally *hairy one*.

with her younger sister, Rachel. And so Leah is trapped in a loveless marriage while simultaneously sharing her husband with her sister. It's not a pretty picture. Scripture tells us that Jacob "loved Rachel more than Leah" (Gen. 29:30). But I assure you that there is more to this story than heartache—much more—because God is with Leah, and it is her sacrifice of praise that paves the way for the next generation in this covenant family. Let's trace Leah's entrance into the story.

In My Father's Footsteps

Scripture records that sometime after Esau sells his birthright to his twin brother Jacob, Isaac moves to a place called Gerar in order to avoid a famine (Gen. 26:1).

> Read Genesis 26:6-7. Compare this passage with Genesis 20:1-2. List all the similarities between them.

It is one thing to literally follow the footsteps of his father Abraham by arriving in Gerar in order to avoid a famine; it is quite another to repeat his father's mistakes while living there. Sadly, like Abraham before him, Isaac, in fear for his life, lies[21] to the local king about his wife, Rebekah. Within each generation, the patterns of sin and deception continue weaving their threads through God's chosen family line. In fact, it will only get worse.

> Optional: read all of Genesis 27 and 28:1-5.

> If God refused to work through imperfect people, who would be left?

In Genesis 27, Rebekah overhears the elderly Isaac's intention of blessing his firstborn and favored son, Esau. Rebekah, however, wants her favorite son Jacob to get the blessing. Taking matters into her own hands, Rebekah gathers some of Esau's garments, along with some goat skins, and convinces Jacob to disguise himself as Esau in order to steal Isaac's blessing—and it works! Lying, stealing, deceiving, manipulating . . . *this* is God's choice for the chosen family line? Yes. After all, if God refused to work through imperfect people, who would be left?

When Esau realizes his brother Jacob stole his blessing, Esau begins plotting to murder Jacob (Gen. 27:41). Rebekah hears of it and once again takes action. With all the drama she can muster, she plants a seed in Isaac's mind to send Jacob away to find a wife from among Rebekah's relatives (Gen. 28:1–5). Today, we will trace Jacob's journey to Haran, where he arrives at the home of his uncle (Rebekah's brother). Once there, we will briefly step into the story of Leah, because without her, there would be no story of Tamar. It is Leah's sacrifice of praise that paves the way for Tamar's entrance into this highly favored, yet decidedly dysfunctional, family.

Day Five / Week One

PAUSE TO PONDER

> Earlier, I asked the rhetorical question: If God refused to work through imperfect people, who would be left? How have you seen this principle at work? How have you seen God work through imperfect people in your own life? How has He worked through *you*?

Jacob's Dream

When we consider the events of Jacob's life up to this point, his actions leave much to be desired. He manipulates his brother into giving him his birthright, and he then tricks his father into giving him his brother's blessing. When he learns that his brother Esau is planning to kill him, Jacob leaves home and heads toward Haran, where his uncle Laban lives. But something extraordinary happens on the way. God speaks to Jacob in a dream. Let's take a look.

Read Genesis 28:10-14.

Despite Jacob's deceptions and trickery, God passes the covenant promises, originally given to Abraham, then Isaac, to Jacob. On the chart on page 247, cross out the name of the firstborn, Esau, and write the name Jacob above "Isaac."

Do you find God's choice surprising? Why or why not?

Read Genesis 28:20-22 (optional: read Gen. 28:10-22). How does Jacob respond to God's blessing?

What does Jacob's response suggest about his relationship with God prior to this point? (Hint: compare Gen. 28:20-21 with Gen. 27:20.)

Anticipating God's Fulfillment

PAUSE TO PONDER

> Think of a time when you personally experienced God's blessing despite an obvious failure on your part. How were you blessed? How else did God use the situation? For example, were others also blessed, or perhaps God opened a door to share the gospel?

The Bait and Switch

After Jacob vows to follow the Lord, he arrives in Haran. There he soon meets his cousin Rachel, who then runs to inform her father, Laban (Rebekah's brother).

Read Genesis 29:13-20 (optional: read Gen. 29:1-20). Briefly summarize the events.

Next, read Genesis 29:21-25. After Jacob completed his seven years of service to his uncle, whom did he ask for, according to verse 21?

Consider the text carefully. In addition to the strong likelihood that Leah would have been wearing a veil, what else may have contributed to Jacob's failure to identify her before morning?

This was quite a ruse. No detail was left to chance. Laban plans a celebratory feast, and that means wine and lots of it.[22] The bride is nowhere to be seen. She is brought to Jacob "in the evening" (Gen. 29:23), suggesting that the party started long before this (as did the flowing of the wine). It is also getting dark. On top of that, the bride would have been veiled. Not only was it customary for an unmarried woman to veil herself in the presence of her future husband[23] (see Gen. 24:64-67), but brides were also fully covered and veiled at their wedding until the marriage was consummated.[24] Last, let's not forget that Jacob had been waiting seven years; it's not surprising that he would have been eager to have his bride—a bit too eager,

Day Five / Week One

perhaps, since he failed to notice the switch. Jacob's failure to ask for his bride by name made it all the easier for Laban to complete his deception.

If you're like me, you might be shaking your head at this point, thinking, "Did Jacob not even *speak* to her?" He likely did, but perhaps Leah said little or nothing at all, or Jacob simply fell asleep. We might be tempted to roll our eyes at this point, but let us give the man some credit; after all, he did wait for her—*seven long years!* I don't know about you, but it seems difficult to imagine that there are many men (or women) today who would be willing to wait so long to have the one they love.

PAUSE TO PONDER

Describe a time when you waited a long time for something that meant a lot to you. What helped you the most during that season of waiting? What did you learn while in the "waiting room"?

What Goes Around Comes Around

Finish the scene by reading Genesis 29:26-30.

No matter how you slice it, this triangle is a tragedy in the making. Both Leah and Rachel would have had no choice in the matter. This was clearly their father's doing. Not only did he find a husband for both his daughters, but he managed to wrangle another seven years of labor out of Jacob.

Glance back at verse 25. What does Jacob accuse Laban of?

Compare this with Jacob's willingness to disguise himself and deceive his own father years earlier. Do Jacob's accusations seem reasonable to you? Why or why not?

What is Laban's explanation for his deception?

Anticipating God's Fulfillment

Compare Laban's explanation with Jacob's demand in Genesis 25:31.

Finally, take a moment to imagine being in Leah's sandals. How might she be feeling? How about Rachel?

On the surface, it all seems so hopeless. Whatever relationship the sisters have, being placed in this impossible situation will all but shatter it. And for Leah, add to that the fact that her husband does not even love her. The word translated *more* in Genesis 29:30 ("he loved Rachel more than Leah") is *mi* in Hebrew. It stems from the root word *min*, meaning *abandon*. Commentary author John Currid explains, "It is not that Jacob loved Rachel more than Leah, but he loved Rachel alone."[25] This is attested to in the next verse.

Write Genesis 29:31 below.

Hate is a strong word in any language. If Jacob's feelings for Leah were neutral prior to discovering her in his bed, it is likely that his feelings changed from that moment, and not for the better. Nevertheless, while Scripture clearly states that "Leah was hated" (Gen. 29:31), there is nothing to suggest that Jacob treated Leah harshly. Instead, the word is meant to express the tragic plight of an unloved wife, especially in contrast to her sister Rachel, whom Jacob loved dearly. In other words, by comparison, Leah would have felt hated. If there were any confusion as to Jacob's feelings for Leah, this verse clears it up.

What reasons may Jacob have had for hating Leah?

Do you think his feelings were justified? Why or why not?

> "Under three things the earth trembles; under four it cannot bear up: a slave when he becomes king, and a fool when he is filled with food; an unloved woman when she gets a husband, and a maidservant when she displaces her mistress."
> —Proverbs 30:21-23

Day Five / Week One

It all seems so hopeless, but God was still present. Up to this point, throughout all of Genesis 29—Jacob's arrival in Haran, his seven-year commitment to Laban, his marriage to Leah and then to Rachel—throughout all this time there is not one single mention of God until we reach verse 31: "When the LORD saw . . ." When the Lord *saw*. Oh, what a precious reminder! Our tender Lord sees every heartache and injustice. Not one goes unnoticed by Him. When I read these words, I can't help but think of Hagar two generations before when she was handed over to Abraham (who was already married to Hagar's owner, Sarah). In the midst of her desert of despair, Hagar gives God the beautiful name El Roi, "the God Who Sees Me" (Gen. 16:13).

Though Leah's circumstances seem hopeless, God sees her pain, but He does more than that. He steps in.

YOUR TURN

Where in your life do you need God to step in right now?

Take a few moments to ask God if there is anything you need to confess or surrender or if there is something He is asking you to do.

What one step can you take as you wait on God to reveal His plan?

Anticipating God's Fulfillment

Lesson Summary

What scripture, statement, or thought was most significant to you this week?*
Write it down, and then reword it into a prayer of response to God.

*Share your favorite takeaway with a friend or on social media using #TamarBibleStudy. At the end of each week, I will share a worship song that you may enjoy. This week's song is called "Yes, I Will," by Vertical Worship.

Notes

[1] *ESV Study Bible* (Wheaton, IL: Crossway Bibles, 2008), 46.

[2] For a more in-depth exploration into the first three chapters of Genesis, you may enjoy Week One, "Reflecting on God's Risk," in my Bible study, *Legion: Rediscovering the God Who Rescues Me* (Abilene, TX: Leafwood Publishers, 2019).

[3] John Calvin and John King, *Commentary on the First Book of Moses Called Genesis*, vol. 1 (Bellingham, WA: Logos Bible Software, 2010), 189.

[4] John D. Currid, *A Study Commentary on Genesis: Genesis 1:1–25:18*, vol. 1, EP Study Commentary (Darlington, UK: Evangelical Press, 2003), 146.

[5] Scot McKnight, "Cain," in *Dictionary of the Old Testament: Pentateuch*, ed. T. Desmond Alexander and David W. Baker (Downers Grove, IL: InterVarsity Press, 2003), 110.

[6] Currid, *A Study Commentary on Genesis*, 158.

[7] This list is not exhaustive. Other Old Testament verses in which God is described as Father to His people include Deuteronomy 32:6; Isaiah 63:16, 64:8; Jeremiah 31:9.

[8] See Matt. 5:9, 5:45; Luke 6:35, 20:36; John 1:12, 1:13, 11:52; Rom. 8:14, 8:15, 8:16, 8:19, 8:21, 9:8, 9:26; Gal. 3:26; Phil. 2:15; 1 John 2:29, 3:1, 3:2, 3:9, 3:10, 4:7, 5:1, 5:2, 5:4, 5:18; Rev. 21:7.

[9] Jesus quotes this passage in John 10:34–35, where he equates the subject in Psalm 82:6 with those "to whom the word of God came"—that is, the leaders/judges of Israel. The Hebrew word being translated in Psalm 82:6 is *elohim*—the same word translated as "judges" in Exodus 21:6 and 22:8 in the KJV, NKJV, and NIV Bible translations. "The judges, to whom the quotation in [John 10] ver. 35 refers, were called gods, as being representatives of God.... Jesus' course of reasoning is, if these judges could be called gods, how do I blaspheme in calling myself Son of God." Marvin Richardson Vincent, *Word Studies in the New Testament*, vol. 2 (New York: Charles Scribner's Sons, 1889), 198.

[10] Even here, there is some debate among scholars.

[11] A few worth mentioning include John Peter Lange et al., *A Commentary on the Holy Scriptures: Genesis* (Bellingham, WA: Logos Bible Software, 2008), 283; John Calvin and John King, *Commentary on the First Book of Moses Called Genesis*, vol. 1 (Bellingham, WA: Logos

Bible Software, 2010), 238; Robert Hawker, *Poor Man's Old Testament Commentary: Genesis–Numbers*, vol. 1 (Bellingham, WA: Logos Bible Software, 2013), 30.

[12] After the flood, God would warn the Israelites over and over again not to intermarry with the surrounding nations, giving further weight to the interpretation of Genesis 6 as being the mixture of God's holy people with those who would turn their hearts against God and His good intent for humanity.

[13] Nowhere, however, does Scripture state that the Nephilim were descended from a mixed race of spiritual and human beings. Further, if the Nephilim were a mixed race of spiritual and human beings, they would not have existed after the flood since they would have been destroyed, but that would contradict verse 4, which states that they did exist after the flood.

[14] It is important to note that the curse was placed on Canaan, not Ham. In years past, some interpreters have distorted the meaning of the text in order to perpetuate a supposed "curse of Ham" (which is not ever mentioned in the text). This supposed "curse of Ham" was then twisted into a justification for the tragic and horrific enslavement of Africans. For a full discussion of this historic interpretation, see David M. Whitford, *The Curse of Ham in the Early Modern Era* (Farnham, UK: Ashgate, 2009). The true outcome of the curse of Canaan (son of Ham) would play out years later as some of the descendants of Canaan settled in the cities of Sodom and Gomorrah, which God would later destroy because of their wickedness (Gen. 10:19–20; see also chapters 18–19).

[15] See Gen. 10:25, 11:10–26.

[16] For a rich exploration into the beautiful story of God's care for Hagar and her son, I encourage you to read my Bible study *Hagar: Rediscovering the God Who Sees Me* (Abilene, TX: Leafwood Publishers, 2017).

[17] See Gen. 12:10–20 and 20:1–18.

[18] In Genesis 22, God describes Isaac as Abraham's "only son." To understand this concept further, see my Bible study *Hagar*.

[19] The allusion to the symbolism in the Lord's Supper is hard to miss—it reminds us of the ultimate price of Jesus offering Himself.

[20] William MacDonald, *Believer's Bible Commentary: Old and New Testaments*, ed. Arthur Farstad (Nashville: Thomas Nelson, 1995), 62.

[21] Some might argue that Abraham's lie was "less" grievous since Sarah was his half-sister, whereas Rebekah was Isaac's cousin. Nevertheless, the motivation in both cases was to deceive the king—even being willing to place their wives at risk.

[22] While it is true that wine at that time was far less potent, this was a daylong celebration (the first of seven days), and wine would have been flowing freely.

[23] Martin H. Manser, *Dictionary of Bible Themes: The Accessible and Comprehensive Tool for Topical Studies* (London: Martin Manser, 2009).

[24] Richard R. Losch, *All the People in the Bible: An A–Z Guide to the Saints, Scoundrels, and Other Characters in Scripture* (Grand Rapids: William B. Eerdmans, 2008), 362.

[25] John D. Currid, *A Study Commentary on Genesis: Genesis 25:19–50:26*, vol. 2, EP Study Commentary (Darlington, UK; Evangelical Press, 2003), 84.

NOTES

NOTES

NOTES

MARVELING AT FORBEARANCE

WEEK TWO

THIS WEEK WE WILL WITNESS THE COURAGE OF JACOB'S unloved wife as she turns from seeking her husband's praise to praising the eternal God. She gives birth to her son, Judah, whose name sounds like the Hebrew word for *praise*.

Sadly, Judah's early years are far from praiseworthy. After selling his brother into slavery and lying to his father to cover up the crime, Judah abandons his family, as well as God's covenant promises. He rejects God's command and marries outside the family. His choice? A Canaanite—a people notorious for their gross immorality and pagan worship.[1] When Judah decides his firstborn son is ready to marry, Tamar steps onto the scene and into God's grand redemptive story.

DAY ONE
Giving God a Sacrifice of Praise

I have always loved puzzles. My mother once told me that when I was a child, whenever she would buy me a puzzle, all she had to do was walk into another room, come back, and it would be finished. (She would then have to go buy me a new one.) I imagine everyone has a different approach to puzzles (I have some friends who would rather avoid them altogether), but I love puzzles. And I love

order. For me, the first steps when starting a new puzzle are always the same: gather all the border pieces, pick out the four corner pieces, and then get to work on laying out the frame of the puzzle. Only after the border is completed will I set to work on the rest of the puzzle.

In preparing for Tamar's entrance into the story, we have been piecing together the big picture—the outline in which her story appears. At the end of last week's lesson, I mentioned that we had two last stops to make. The first is the story of Leah, which we will finish today. Tomorrow, we will explore the story of Judah and his brothers' betrayal of their younger brother, Joseph, which appears immediately prior to Genesis 38, where Tamar first appears in the narrative. This will be the last puzzle piece that completes the framework, providing us with a vivid backdrop in which we will witness the unfolding of Tamar's story and God's redemption.

What Defines Your Worth?

In biblical times, having children, especially sons, was considered the highest honor for a woman. In contrast, to be barren was often viewed as a curse from God. From a human perspective, a woman's worth was measured by her beauty and ability to produce children.

> Read Genesis 29:31-35, and answer the questions (verse 31 is a review). What words or phrases reveal Leah's emotions in the passage?

In the first column below, list the name of each of Leah's sons in the order of their birth. In the last column, state the reason she chose each name. I completed the first name for you. I have also included a middle column with the background of each name in case that information is not provided in your Bible's footnotes.

Son's Name	Background of Name[2]	Reason She Chose the Name
Reuben	It means "See, a son."	The Lord looked upon her affliction (and she believed Jacob would now love her).
	It sounds like "heard."	
	It sounds like "attached."	
	It sounds like "praise."	

Day One / Week Two

How did Leah cope with her sorrow?

How did God bless Leah, and how did Leah respond?

What might Leah's responses reveal about her character and relationship with God?

 What other observations can you make?

A Sacrifice of Praise

My heart aches for Leah. There is perhaps nothing more tragic than a person desperately trying to earn someone's love. But in the midst of Leah's heartache we see something else: a soul crying out to God. With each of her sons' entrance into the world, we see Leah's heart reaching out to the Lord. She is not alone, and she knows this because the Lord is mentioned in all but one verse! Despite her pain and sorrow and the impossible situation that was forced upon her, Leah made a choice to not only acknowledge, but to praise God through it all. What a testimony of faith!

> Despite our pain and sorrow and any impossible situation forced upon us, like Leah, we can choose to acknowledge and praise God through it all.

PAUSE TO PONDER

Consider a time when you made the choice to give God praise despite painful circumstances. How was this a sacrifice (costly to you)? How might your sacrifice have been pleasing to God? What one thing can you give God praise for that happened within the past week?

Marveling at God's Forbearance

"Most hurt feelings are the result of unmet expectations."[3] —Kendra Burrows

After years of longing for her husband's affection, Leah made the choice to give a sacrifice of praise to God. Imagine how that must have blessed God's heart. Leah gave birth to her fourth son and named him Judah, which sounds like the Hebrew word for *praise*. But the story doesn't end there. All this time, Leah's sister Rachel is barren—a painful stigma for a woman in that culture. One woman yearning for love and the other yearning for children, both suffering the despair of unmet expectations.

PAUSE TO PONDER

> Where in your life right now are you struggling with unmet expectations? How can you sympathize with Leah and/or Rachel? What can you do to guard yourself against despair or resentment when you face unmet expectations?

Read Genesis 30:1-2. Compare and contrast Jacob's response to Rachel with his father Isaac's response in Genesis 25:21 when Isaac and Rebekah faced barrenness a generation earlier.

What does each man's response reveal about his relationship with God?

    Isaac:

    Jacob:

Next, read Genesis 30:1-13, and briefly summarize the events.

Day One / Week Two

When Rachel sees she has no other option and Jacob fails to invite God into the matter, Rachel resolves to take matters into her own hands. In desperation, she follows in the footsteps of Jacob's grandmother, Sarah. Handing her servant to Jacob, Rachel orders[4] Jacob to use her servant to produce a child, which Rachel would claim as her own. Even Rachel's words mirror those of Sarah.

Read Genesis 16:2, and note its similarities to Genesis 30:3.

Desperate for a family, both Sarah and Rachel use their servant to produce a child on their behalf.[5] However, the original wording is even more telling. In both passages, Sarah and Rachel are quoted using the same root Hebrew word, *banah*. The word sounds like the Hebrew word for *son* (pronounced "ben"), but it literally means *to build*. Each woman is determined to build a family through any means possible.

Instead of trusting in God's plan, the women each took matters into their own hands. Jacob now has four women to contend with—a far cry from God's intended design ("[the two] shall become one flesh" [Gen. 2:24]).

PAUSE TO PONDER

> Think of a time when you wanted something badly enough that you were willing to use another person to get it. What was the outcome? What did you gain, and what did you lose?

Rachel's decision to use her servant sets off a chain reaction, whereby Leah follows suit, giving her servant to Jacob as well, and not just once, as was the case with Sarah using Hagar. Rather, Jacob fathered two sons with each servant. But it gets even worse!

Read Genesis 30:14-18. What two or three words would you use to describe Leah's perception of Rachel?

Marveling at God's Forbearance

Compare Genesis 29:26 with Genesis 30:16. How does Leah seem to view her relationship with Jacob?

How does God respond to Leah's actions, according to Genesis 30:17?

Do you find God's response surprising? Confusing? Share your thoughts.

Four women; one man. To say that there was jealousy and conflict would be quite the understatement. One day, it nears the point of absurdity when Rachel strikes a bargain with her sister to buy Leah's mandrakes as payment for Jacob's services—talk about family dysfunction!

This is the household that Judah is growing up in.

Why Mandrakes?

Mandrakes still grow today near Jerusalem and in other parts of Palestine. It is a flowering plant that produces a pale orange fruit, which was believed to be both an aphrodisiac and enhancer of fertility.[7] No wonder both women were eager to have its fruit—one because she was suffering the heartache of an unloved wife; the other because she was suffering the shame and grief of barrenness. But God is merciful, and He loves them both. He blesses each of them, who, together, bear Jacob several more sons.

.....................YOUR TURN.....................

Is there a relationship in which you long for love? Perhaps an estranged spouse, family member, or friend? In what way(s) can you sympathize with Leah?

> *Mandrakes* is a word stemming from the Hebrew word *dod*, meaning *beloved*. Because of its narcotic properties, it is sometimes referred to as a "love apple." Among Arabs, it is called "Satan's apple."[6]

What is one lesson you have learned from Leah's experience that you could apply to your life?

Read John 15:9, John 16:27, and Ephesians 2:4-5, and choose one to rewrite into a prayer of thanksgiving to God.

Day Two
Yearning for the Father's Love

Today we will cover the last stop on the timeline leading up to Tamar's entrance into the Genesis narrative. It's the story of Jacob's sons. All in all, Jacob fathered twelve sons, but none captured his heart more than his young son, Joseph. In the same way that Jacob's own parents, Isaac and Rebekah, each favored one son, Jacob favored Joseph. He favored him so much that Joseph's brothers eventually came to hate the boy.

Read Genesis 37:1-36 to get an overview of the story. Then, summarize the reason(s) for the underlying conflict between Joseph and his brothers, according to verses 1-11.

One of a Kind

Hanging in my hall closet is a stylish black leather jacket that I have had for nearly twenty years. Though it is old, it has always been my favorite. I remember the first year I had it, I wore it often—maybe too often. Every now and then a stranger would stop to offer a compliment. Sometimes they would ask the name of the designer. My answer was always the same: "I don't know, but it is one of a kind."

Marveling at God's Forbearance

Years ago, I was given the jacket by a family friend who worked in designer fashions in New York City. Part of her job was managing the countless fashion shows scheduled throughout the year. After every show, it was her job to collect any discarded "samples"—unwanted clothing that was featured in the show but did not sell. The samples were often simply given away to friends or family, but not until the labels were removed. My jacket was one of those samples, and when it was offered to me, I was delighted to discover that it was a perfect fit! The fact that it is one of a kind adds to its appeal. To this day, I don't know who the designer is, but it is still my favorite.

Playing Favorites

Joseph is somewhat famous for his robe of many colors, which was also one of a kind. Not only that, but he enjoyed the added blessing of knowing that his own father made (or had it made) for him. Perhaps he enjoyed his father's favor, and his fancy robe, a bit too much. Like my leather jacket, Joseph's robe also attracted attention. Joseph's eagerness to flaunt his dreams of ruling over his brothers likely didn't help matters.

No one is entirely certain about the garment's features or even if it had multiple colors. The phrase being translated from Hebrew can also mean that the robe (tunic) had long sleeves or was ornately designed. Whatever Jacob made for Joseph, it was special—so special that Joseph's brothers could recognize him coming, even from a distance.

> "But if you have bitter jealousy and selfish ambition in your hearts, do not boast and be false to the truth. This is not the wisdom that comes down from above, but is earthly, unspiritual, demonic."
> —James 3:14-15

In general, how would you rate your view of jealousy or envy? Mark an X on the line below.

_____
not serious   very serious

Read James 3:14-15 in the margin. What is God's view of jealousy? Mark an X on the line below.

_____
not serious   very serious

Compare your view of jealousy with God's. Are they the same? Different? Share your thoughts.

Day Two / Week Two

PAUSE TO PONDER

> Reflect on a time when you personally experienced jealousy of or a rivalry with another person. What was the underlying cause? How did you handle your feelings? How did you handle the situation? What did you learn?

Glance back at Genesis 37:18–24. Briefly describe the events.

As Joseph approaches, his brothers come up with a plan. Today we would call it what it is: premeditated murder. However, before they can carry out their plan, the firstborn among the brothers, Reuben, tries to intervene. On the surface, it seems that Reuben's actions are noble, but he may have had other motives. Commentary author Steven Carpenter suggests, "As the oldest, Reuben would be held accountable to Jacob for Joseph's life."[8] Whatever Reuben's motive, he quickly falls into the background as Judah enters the scene.

Unpraiseworthy

Glance back at Genesis 37:25–28. Then answer the questions that follow.

What does Judah propose?

List two or three motives that may have driven Judah's actions.

What does the brothers' response suggest about Judah's influence and the dynamics among the brothers?

Marveling at God's Forbearance

Do you think that Judah's actions were honorable? Dishonorable? Explain.

Overstepping the firstborn Reuben (who had departed), Judah assumes leadership of the band of brothers by proposing a different plan only slightly less vile than their original aim to kill the boy. As with Reuben, at this point it is not yet entirely clear whether Judah's motives are honorable (seeking to save his brother's life) or dishonorable (seeking to get rid of the pesky brother while making a profit at the same time). However, there are some insights we can glean from the context, including what is not stated in the text.

What did the brothers do immediately after throwing Joseph into the empty pit? What does this suggest about their hearts?

> "Search me, O God, and know my heart! Try me and know my thoughts! And see if there be any grievous way in me, and lead me in the way everlasting!"
> —Psalm 139:23-24

When Judah and his brothers sold Joseph to the traders,⁹ what did the brothers do? Circle all that apply.

- They asked the traders for assurance that Joseph would not be harmed.
- They provided Joseph with food and clothing for the journey.
- They asked to be sent word where in Egypt they could later find Joseph.
- They collected twenty shekels of silver.

How may the brothers' indifference concerning Joseph's future offer further insight into their hearts?

In Leviticus 27:5, twenty shekels of silver was the value required to redeem a male person between the ages of five and twenty, which would have been based on the price of slaves at that time. Seeing an opportunity for material gain, Judah proposes a way to avoid the burden of having Joseph's death on their consciences. As an added bonus, they will pocket twenty shekels of silver. "Judah's real concern

Day Two / Week Two

is not so much to save his brother from death as to save himself from guilt,"[10] and make a little money on the side.

Instead of facing their father, Judah and the brothers convince messengers (perhaps family servants) to send the bloody robe back to Jacob and lie to him by saying that they had found it. The grammatical construction of Genesis 37:32 is: "And they sent the robe of many colors and [*they* (new subject; i.e., the messengers by whom the brothers sent the robe)] brought it to their father and said, 'This we have found...'" *The JPS Torah Commentary* authors explain, "Hoping to avoid any suspicion of involvement in Joseph's fate, the brothers apparently sent the bloodstained tunic to their father by way of others who pretended they had found it."[11] This helps clarify why the messengers would refer to Joseph as "your son" rather than "our brother."

Here we get our first glimpse into Judah's character, and it falls far short of his name (which sounds like "praise" in Hebrew). Together with his brothers, he conspires to kill young Joseph, after which they strip him of his fancy robe and throw him into a pit. Thinking nothing of breaking their father's heart, they sell the boy to strangers as a slave. Murder. Betrayal. Slavery. Deception. These are not the kinds of qualities anyone would want in a brother. This is reminiscent of our first day of study when we explored the glaring contrast in Cain and Abel, the first set of brothers born into the world.

When History Repeats Itself

Try to fill in the blanks from memory. If you need to peek at the passage, reread 1 John 3:12.

> We should not be like Cain, who was of the _____ one
>
> and murdered his _____. And why did he murder him?
>
> Because his own deeds were _____ and his brother's _____.

- Consider 1 John 3:12 above; how are these truths reflected in the story of Joseph and his brothers?

In the table, compare the events of Joseph and his brothers with the story of Cain and Abel. Complete the table by recording the similarities between the two stories. In the left column, I have listed various aspects of their stories. I

Marveling at God's Forbearance

included the Scripture references, if you need them, at the top of the columns. I completed the first one for you.

	Cain and Abel (Gen. 4:2-11)	**Joseph and His Brothers** (Gen. 37:2-36)
Source of conflict	God looks favorably on Abel's offering but has no regard for Cain's.	Jacob shows special favor to Joseph over his brothers.
Events (What happened?)		
Motivation (Why did it happen?)		
Heart condition (Is there remorse?)		
Other		

The parallels between the two stories up to this point are striking, but we're not finished. There is one more key parallel in the story I want to cover. If you're the type of person who enjoys a challenge and wants to guess ahead of time what the last parallel might be, write your answer in the last row marked "Other" on the previous table.

> Reread Genesis 37:2. What else may have helped fuel the conflict between Joseph and his brothers?

Compare and contrast Genesis 37:26-27 and 37:31 with Genesis 4:10-11, which provides the other key parallel I mentioned (perhaps you even noticed others). List the similarities between these verses.

How is the character (or nature) of Cain reflected in the actions of Judah and his brothers?

Stripped of Identity

The specific reference to Joseph's "robe of many colors" occurs three times in the passage. In the space below, briefly describe the events surrounding each reference to Joseph's fancy robe. I completed the first one for you.

Reference	Describe the Events
Genesis 37:3-4	Jacob loved Joseph more than his other sons and made him a fancy robe. Joseph's brothers were jealous for their father's love and therefore hated Joseph.
Genesis 37:23-24	
Genesis 37:31-33	

Joseph's brothers hated him because each of them yearned for their father's love. Who could blame them? Jacob had four women vying for his attention, as well as twelve sons and one daughter (Gen. 30:21[12]), not to mention all kinds of servants, flocks, and herds under his care. To the eleven brothers, Joseph's elaborate robe was a glaring reminder of their father's favor. No wonder the first thing they did was strip Joseph of his garment while wishing they could strip him of their father's love. The ringleader? Judah, the one for whom Leah gave the Lord praise.

································ YOUR TURN ································

Where in your life right now are you yearning for your heavenly Father's love? If you are not sure, take a few moments and ask God to reveal where you might be experiencing despair, discontentment, or discouragement.

Is there someone you envy (or have envied) who seems especially blessed by God? What may be at the root of your envy? Confess your struggle to God, and ask Him to help you see the person through His eyes.

As you consider the above questions, write any specific steps God is asking you to take.

If you are not currently struggling in any of these areas, write a prayer of gratitude, and give praise to God.

DAY THREE
Heading Down the Wrong Path

Perhaps you were already familiar with the story of Judah and his brothers, or maybe you read it yesterday for the first time. The curious thing about these events is that, right in the middle of the ordeal, just when the good guy seems defeated, the author puts the whole thing on pause to tell the story of Tamar and Judah.

Scripture devotes one full chapter (thirty verses) to the story. At first glance, that may not seem like much. After all, there are 1,189 chapters in the Bible. But the Bible is infinitely rich, inspired by an infinite, all-wise, all-knowing God. Each word is there for a reason. When we take our time, careful study of any passage will reveal deep and rewarding truths. As with many passages in Scripture, there is often more going on *behind the seen*.

Going in the Wrong Direction

I am the first to admit I have a terrible sense of direction (anyone who knows me would wholeheartedly agree). A while back, I needed to undergo a minor medical procedure. Because I was going to be given local anesthesia, I was told to arrange for someone to drive me home. My dear friend Liz had recently retired and happily agreed to give me a ride. Being that my appointment would take a little more than an hour, Liz had arranged to visit with a friend who lived nearby until I texted her that I was ready to be picked up.

I had never been to this office before. It was located within a large, white medical building. After Liz dropped me off at the entrance, I entered the building and immediately found the directory. Seeing that the office was only one floor up, I decided to take the stairs. The stark white-walled corridor of the second floor was lined end to end with two dozen identical light oak office doors. I found the suite about halfway down the hall and went inside. An hour later, I was resting in a quiet recovery room, where I texted Liz to let her know I would be ready in fifteen minutes.

When it came time for me to leave, I stepped out of the office and into the hallway. Looking to my right and then to my left, I couldn't remember which end of the hallway I had come up. I hung my head. "You really should pay better attention," I scolded myself. Figuring I had a fifty–fifty chance of getting it right, I headed down the hall and then the stairs. When I exited the building, the door locked behind me before I realized I was not in the front but at a back door. Sigh.

I had no choice but to walk all the way around the building to reach the front, where Liz was waiting. She was parked at the entrance, facing the direction I was walking from. Even through the car windshield, I could see her look up in surprise as I approached. I opened the passenger door and sat down. She looked at me quizzically as if expecting an explanation, but she said nothing. She knows more than anyone my embarrassing history of getting lost.

> Briefly summarize the events we examined previously in Genesis 37 by filling in the blanks using the keywords (I included the Scripture references in case you need them. Note: the statements are not direct quotes but rather a summarized version of the events).

Verse	Keywords: jealous slavery rule blood comforted kill dreamed loved Judah robe mourned
3	Jacob (Israel) _____ Joseph more than any other of his sons.
9-10	Joseph _____ that he would _____ over his parents and brothers.
11, 18	The brothers were _____ of Joseph and conspired to _____ him.
26-27	_____ convinced the brothers to sell Joseph into _____.
31-32	The brothers dipped Joseph's _____ in _____ and sent it to their father.
34-35	Jacob _____ for Joseph and refused to be _____.

"In all your ways acknowledge him, and he will make straight your paths."
—Proverbs 3:6

Marveling at God's Forbearance

> "If we are faithless, he remains faithful—for he cannot deny himself."
>
> —2 Timothy 2:13

If these events were not recorded in Scripture, you and I might have a hard time believing that God's people are capable of such coldhearted actions, but then all we need to do is turn back to Genesis 4 and remember the story of Cain and Abel. If it were not for the fact that God, in His mercy, inserts glimmers of hope in each of these stories, we might risk succumbing to despair. But God never abandons His people—not then, not now—even when we sin and fail.

One of my favorite Bible verses is the sweet reminder in 2 Timothy 2:13, which says that even "if we are faithless, he remains faithful—for he cannot deny himself." What a promise! If we belong to Him, even when we fail Him, He will never abandon us. He cannot because He can never be anything contrary to who He is, which is faithful, loving, kind, holy, and so much more.

PAUSE TO PONDER

> Think of a time when you were faithless but God remained faithful. What impact did it have on your relationship with Him?

Read Genesis 38:1. (Optional: read verses 1-5; we will read the full chapter next week, but for now, I want us to focus on verses 1-5.)

Adullam was another city in Canaan, approximately fifteen miles northwest of Hebron, the Canaanite city where Jacob's family was living. It would have taken Judah perhaps one day to travel from Hebron to Adullam.

List two or three reasons why Judah may have wanted to move away from his brothers.

When you consider Judah's departure, are you sympathetic? Disappointed? Share your thoughts.

Try to imagine being each of the following people. How might Judah's decision to leave have affected you?

Day Three / Week Two

Jacob:

Leah:

One of Judah's brothers:

It Happened at That Time

As the events surrounding Joseph and his brothers fade into the background, Judah takes center stage. The author begins Genesis chapter 38 with these words: "It happened at that time. . . ." What time?

> List what had recently happened to each person below as recorded in Genesis 37. I included the verse references if you need them.
>
> Judah (verses 26-27):
>
>
>
> Jacob (verses 33-35):
>
>
>
> Joseph (verse 36):

Judah "went down from his brothers" (Gen. 38:1) at the time when his father is drowning in grief, at the time when Joseph is being carried off into slavery, at the time when the betrayal is ushered in by Judah's own words. It is *at that time* that Judah decides to leave his family behind.[13]

Marveling at God's Forbearance

PAUSE TO PONDER

> Think back on a time when you did something that caused you to want to distance yourself (either physically or emotionally) from anything or anyone that reminded you of your actions. What was the outcome? What did you learn?

Scripture records that, on his journey, Judah "turned aside to a certain Adullamite . . ." (Gen. 38:1). In English, the sentence seems fairly straightforward, but the verb translated "turned aside" is important.[14] The Hebrew verb is *yet* and implies a change of direction, but it is rarely used in the physical sense, such as toward a person or place. The word is taken from the Hebrew root word *natah*, which primarily means to bend or stretch (as in pitching one's tent, in Genesis 12:8 and elsewhere). However, the word can also mean to incline oneself, such as in the abstract sense. A great example is Joshua 24:23: "Then put away the foreign gods that are among you, and incline your heart to the Lord." The word can also suggest deviating from a path of loyalty or righteousness.[15] In other words, the author wants us to recognize that, for Judah, there is more going on than him physically turning aside to visit a friend. There is a turning aside in a spiritual sense as well; Judah was heading one way, and now he is heading another.

More Wrong Choices

Your word is a lamp to my feet and a light to my path.
Psalm 119:105

There is a reason why God's Word is described as a light to our path. The further we travel in the wrong direction—away from God and His Word—the darker it gets. Once we take that first wrong turn, unless or until we turn around, we will continue walking further into the darkness, making more and more wrong choices.

Read Genesis 38:1-2 (verse 1 is a review). After Judah interacts with a man named Hirah, what happens next?

List what we are told about the woman Judah takes for himself.

Day Three / Week Two

The name *Shua* in Hebrew stems from a root word meaning wealth or riches; the name may also mean opulence, prosperity, or noble (as in being wealthy).[16] This means that Judah's father-in-law would have been a nobleman who was wealthy and prominent.[17]

What led Judah to take the woman, according to the text? Circle your response below. Next, what do you know of her family background? Place a box around all that apply.

> Hirah praised her character.
>
> Judah saw her (her beauty).
>
> God told Judah to marry her.
>
> Her family was wealthy.
>
> Judah knew her and spoke with her.
>
> She was a Canaanite.

In your own words, rewrite the instruction of Abraham, Judah's great-grandfather, and Isaac, Judah's grandfather, as recorded in Genesis 24:2-4 and 28:1.

How do these passages compare with Judah's actions?

What appears to be the motivating force behind Judah's decisions up to this point of his life? Circle one.

> flesh   spirit

What do you think would happen to a person who continues on this path?

Judah would have been well aware of God's covenant promises and His desire to keep the holy line "pure." This would include not marrying or otherwise joining with the people of Canaan (described as "cursed" in Genesis 9:25) and other nations. God had good reasons to keep them separate. Moses would later write

Marveling at God's Forbearance

them as a command for God's people in Deuteronomy and Exodus.[18] Let's take a quick look.

Read Deuteronomy 7:1-4 and Exodus 34:12-16, and then answer the questions:

What is prohibited?

Why is it prohibited?

Why does it matter? (Hint: see Ezra 9:1-2.)

When Judah decides to marry a Canaanite, he "abandons the restrictions of the covenant into which he was born."[19] He is not interested in following in the footsteps of Abraham or Isaac, or even his father Jacob, who married within his tribal family (even if he did get tangled up in polygamy). Judah shows no regard for the privileged path God has laid out for his family. Instead, he decides to go his own way.

............................YOUR TURN............................

If we are faithless, he remains faithful—for he cannot deny himself.

2 Timothy 2:13

Reflect on the past week; where have you deviated from God's path?

If you are still on this path, what do you risk if you continue in this direction?

If you are no longer on this path, what helped you turn around?

Take a few moments to seek God in prayer. Is there something you need to ask from God? Is there something you want to thank Him for? Write a prayer as He leads.

DAY FOUR
Being Called by His Name

Yesterday, we finished our lesson with the realization that Judah had stepped away from the covenant path God established for His family by marrying a Canaanite woman. It seems that Judah preferred to make his own decisions—to do things his own way. Sadly, this is a mindset that all of us can relate to at one time or another.

Equally, Then Unequally, Yoked

When I married my former spouse, neither of us were Christians. Each of us came to the relationship carrying a heavy bag of all kinds of dysfunction. For fourteen years, our dysfunctions "worked" together. He was a volatile alcoholic, and I was a codependent enabler. A perfect fit, or, I should say, a perfect storm. Though our relationship was plagued with abuse and chaos, we stayed together. Our unhealthy patterns had become familiar, and familiar eventually becomes comfortable. Imagine how this must grieve God's heart! He designed marriage to be a reflection of His love for us; oh, how we fall so short!

When I was in seminary, I took a class by a professor who was also a licensed counselor. One day, he talked about the simple but tragic truth that emotionally unhealthy people form relationships with other emotionally unhealthy people. A dear friend of mine says it even more succinctly: "Wounded people attract wounded people." Ouch. When I first became a Christian, I was still unaware that I needed healing. I expected God would miraculously heal my marriage, but that didn't happen. However, in time, through counseling and loving prayer support, I no longer responded to the cycle of dysfunction as I once did. But my husband

> It's a common but tragic truth: wounded people attract wounded people.

was not interested in change; he was content with the way things had always been. We had become "unequally yoked." As a result, the behavioral cycle broke, and my husband left and filed for divorce.

Looking back, it seems strange to consider that when I was on the wrong path, my marriage somehow "worked" (it was severely unhealthy, but we stayed together).[20] Only after God shined His light into my heart and led me onto the right path did I come to recognize how dysfunctional our marriage had been. The divorce was a painful season of my life, especially as a baby Christian. But through it all, God was teaching me of His faithfulness, His mercy, and His love. He never left me, even when I failed Him (and oh, how I failed Him!).

To this day, He remains faithful, no matter what.

Read 2 Corinthians 6:14 in the margin. What does it mean to be "unequally yoked"?

> "Do not be unequally yoked with unbelievers. For what partnership has righteousness with lawlessness? Or what fellowship has light with darkness?"
> —2 Corinthians 6:14

Why is it important to avoid being "unequally yoked"?

Compare and contrast 2 Corinthians 6:14 with God's command in the Old Testament to keep His people separated from other nations (see Deuteronomy 7:3-4 and Exodus 34:12-16, which we explored yesterday). What is God's ultimate aim? (Hint: see 2 Corinthians 6:16b-18 and Ezra 9:1-2.)

PAUSE TO PONDER

Have you (or someone you care about) ever experienced being "unequally yoked"? What specific challenges did you face? How did you overcome them? What advice would you give to someone considering such an arrangement?

Read Genesis 38:1-5 (verses 1-2 are a review), and briefly describe the events.

Genesis 38 begins at a rapid pace. Much is happening in those first few verses. By the time we arrive at verse 6 (which we will cover momentarily), Judah and his wife have three sons. Even more, Judah's firstborn is now old enough to marry.

Names Matter

Ever since I sensed God's call to serve Him through writing, I have attended a number of Christian writers conferences. One thing I learned over the years is that when you sit next to someone who you don't know at a conference, it's a great idea to ask the person what they enjoy writing about. I can't count how many wonderful friendships I have developed at these conferences over the years—most of them starting over a conversation at dinner.

There's one particular evening several years ago that I will never forget. I arrived late to the crowded dining hall. I scanned the room, and there was scarcely an empty seat to be found. Finally, tucked back in a corner, I spied a couple of empty chairs at a table where several women had already started eating their dinner. I quickly filled my dinner plate at the buffet line and weaved my way through the crowded room until I reached the table. I asked the women if I could join them. They nodded, kindly motioning for me to sit down.

After I set down my dinner and tucked my computer bag under my chair, I turned to the woman next to me and prepared to introduce myself. I noticed she wasn't wearing a name badge. "That's okay," I thought to myself. "Maybe this is her first conference; I'll start. Hi. I'm Shadia. So, what do you write?" She smiled and began to describe some of her books. She then asked me about my writing. I told her how I had recently published a Bible study for women seeking hope and healing after abortion, in which I share my own personal story.[21]

Immediately, she began telling me about her passion for the sanctity of human life. I was delighted to discover we had something in common. When she began describing a certain novel she had written centered on this topic, I realized she was referring to a book I had at home in my "to read" pile. That's when it finally clicked. "You're Francine Rivers!" I blurted a bit too loud. I was talking to one of the most famous Christian fiction authors on the planet and didn't even know it! Because Francine is not the type of person who seeks attention for herself, she simply smiled.

Marveling at God's Forbearance

Our conversation that evening eventually blossomed into a friendship that I treasure to this day. I can only wonder: Had I known who she was before I sat down, would I have hesitated to intrude? Would I have said something different? Would I have remained quiet? Truly, God orchestrated that little encounter. Looking back, I'm glad she wasn't wearing a name badge.

PAUSE TO PONDER

> Consider Proverbs 22:1 printed in the margin. How would you explain this principle, in your own words, to a friend? How have you witnessed its truth in your own experience?

"A good name is to be chosen rather than great riches, and favor is better than silver or gold."

—Proverbs 22:1

Who's Your Daddy?

In biblical times, one's ancestry was of utmost importance. Throughout the Bible, in addition to extensive genealogies (the ancients kept detailed records!), you will often find that a person is introduced by referencing the name of the person's father or ancestor.

Look once more at Genesis 38:2. Now, skip ahead and read Genesis 38:6. In the table, compare and contrast the description of the two women. What specific information is provided about each woman? What information is left out?

	What We Are Told	**What Is Omitted**
Judah's wife		
Er's wife		

What reason(s) might the writer have had for choosing to include certain details over others when introducing each woman?

Day Four / Week Two

The only description we have of Judah's wife relates to who her father is. He is a Canaanite, and his name (or family name) is Shua. She is mentioned once more in 1 Chronicles 2:3, which reads, "The sons of Judah: Er, Onan and Shelah; these three Bath-shua the Canaanite bore to him." The reference to Bath-shua in 1 Chronicles is not her name. *Bath* is the Hebrew word for daughter; Bath-shua simply means "the daughter of Shua." The principal detail the author wants to emphasize concerning her identity is the fact that she is Canaanite.

However, when Tamar enters the scene, we are not told her nationality, her ancestry, or even the name of her closest male relative. We can speculate that she was Canaanite. This is a reasonable assumption held by a number of scholars,[23] but apparently the author did not consider her nationality or family origins relevant—a curious omission when one's family of origin was considered of utmost importance in those days. Instead, we are given one detail: her name.

Right from the start, we see a stark contrast between how these two women are introduced in the narrative. With the first, her nationality and ancestry are recorded, but her name is left out; for the second, her nationality and ancestry are left out, but her name is forever etched in God's holy Word.

Oh, I can hardly wait to dive into the details of Tamar's story, but first, we need to finish our study of verses 1–5, as these provide critical context for what lies ahead.

A Hidden Meaning

The events that follow the introduction of Judah's wife are bluntly summarized in the passage. In fact, the author barely pauses between them.

> In the space below, list the names of each of Judah's three sons in the order of their birth and who named each one, according to Genesis 38:3–5.

Son's name	Who names him?
Firstborn:	
Second born:	

> The Hebrew name Tamar (*tmr*) means date palm or palm tree.[22]

Third born:	

🖋 Consider Judah's involvement in the naming of his three sons. Why might the author have included this information? What might it suggest about Judah's interest in each son?

Fun Fact: Er's name is pronounces *Eye-er* in Hebrew, with the emphasis on the first syllable.

After Judah takes (marries) the Canaanite's daughter, she immediately conceives and bears Judah's firstborn. Judah steps right in and names his son. Then his wife bears two more sons, but Judah leaves his wife to choose the names for the other two. The author included this information for a reason. While there is nothing to suggest that Judah didn't love and care for all of his sons, his naming of his firstborn and not the others may imply at least some special interest in his firstborn son. This would not be surprising given that firstborn sons were highly esteemed in that time and culture.

> Recall what we learned in the story of twin brothers Jacob and Esau. What special benefits could the firstborn son expect to enjoy? (Hint: glance back at page 44.)

You have done a lot of work in this study up to this point. Today and tomorrow's lessons are intentionally a bit lighter, giving you the opportunity to catch up if you need to before we dive into Week Three, where Tamar makes her first entrance into the story. Tomorrow, we will finish our overview of Genesis 38:1–5 by examining the names of Judah's three sons. Each one serves a purpose in the narrative. Curiously, unlike the names of Judah's second and third sons, the meaning of the name of Judah's firstborn, Er, is uncertain, but even his name turns out to be telling. Stay tuned.

Day Four / Week Two

......................YOUR TURN......................

*Yet you, O Lord, are in the midst of us,
and we are called by your name.*

Jeremiah 14:9b

Scripture teaches us that, as God's people, we are called by His name (Isaiah 43:7, Jeremiah 14:9, and Acts 15:17, to name a few).

> Reflect on the past week; describe two or three ways that being called by His name has made a difference in your life.

> How will you glorify His name this week?

> If you have never made the decision to be called by the name of the Lord by becoming a follower of Jesus, what might be holding you back?

DAY FIVE
Entangled in a Web of Deception

One weekend after an evening church service, my friend Jennifer and I decided to go out for dinner. Several weeks had passed since she and I had seen one another, and we had much catching up to do. We decided to drive to a new shopping center that had recently opened. After we arrived and parked the car, we began walking along the storefronts, chatting as we went. We paused in front of a restaurant to read the menu posted by the front door. It looked promising: fish tacos, savory chicken with ginger, beef with sautéed vegetables . . . mmmm, sounded good!

We strolled inside the restaurant, still chatting about that evening's church service. The hostess smiled as she greeted us and motioned for us to follow her. As she led us to one of the few remaining open tables, she mentioned something about the menu, but my friend and I were too engaged in conversation to pay much attention. Besides, we had already seen the one posted outside.

After we were settled in our seats and had time to look over the menu, a waiter came by to take our order. I asked about an item on the menu, curious if the chicken was white or dark meat. "What kind of chicken is it?"

"It's soy."

I was confused. Maybe he meant the chicken was raised on soy. So I asked about the fish tacos. "What kind of fish is it?"

"It's soy."

Seeing the perplexed look on my face, he explained that the hostess should have informed us that we were in a vegetarian restaurant. Now I was really confused. I pointed to the menu. "But it says you have chicken and fish and beef."

"It's soy. Those are all soy."

Apparently, I failed to notice that beef, chicken, and fish were all in quote marks on the menu. Finally, I ordered the only thing on the menu I felt I could trust: the eggplant. It turned out to be delicious, but I couldn't help but wonder, why call something chicken if it's not chicken? Or beef or fish, for that matter? I get it now: it was a vegan restaurant, but why not just say what it is so a distracted soul like myself, who also happens to be painfully literal, is not left confused? Why fabricate a menu to look like something it isn't? Just tell us what it is. Serving vegan? Great! Be proud; own it!

"Deliver me, O Lord, from lying lips, from a deceitful tongue." —Psalm 120:2

PAUSE TO PONDER

For fun, share a memorable story when you encountered misleading information or misunderstood what was being communicated to you. What was the outcome? If there was a lesson learned, what was it?

What's in a Name?

Yesterday, we learned that Judah and his wife had three sons. Although the meaning of the name of Judah's firstborn son is unknown, that is not the case with the names of his other two sons. The name of Judah's second born, Onan, means *vigorous*.[24] The name of his third born, Shelah, stems from the Hebrew word *shalah*, which means *quiet* and suggests an element of deception.[25]

In Scripture, often the meaning of a person's name is important as it can provide additional insight into the person or events of his or her life. In the table, I have provided the meaning of the names (or the word the name sounds like) of several people in the Bible. Using the Scripture references, fill in the missing names in the second column. I completed two for you.

In the last column, consider each Scripture reference, and record why the meaning of the name (or the word it sounds like) is significant for each person. I completed two for you.

Scripture	Person's Name	Meaning of the Name (or What It Sounds Like)	Significance
Genesis 17:4-6	Abraham	father of a multitude	God promised He would make Abraham into a multitude of nations.
Genesis 16:11		God hears	
Genesis 29:35		praise	
Ruth 1:16-17	Ruth	friendship	Ruth committed herself to Naomi, vowing that only death would separate them.

Most everyone has given a name to someone or something at one time or another. We might be tasked with choosing a name for our child(ren) or our pets. When we were younger, perhaps we had a name for a favorite childhood toy or imaginary friend. When I was twelve, I was given a diary. At the time, I was struggling to fit in at school and was often teased because of my uncommon name. I still have that little yellow diary. Instead of "Dear diary," every entry begins with "Dear Laura." I dreamed of changing my name to Laura, and giving that name to my diary was as close as I could get.

Marveling at God's Forbearance

PAUSE TO PONDER

> Chances are that at some time in your life, you chose a name for someone or something. Why did you choose the name you chose? What significance did it have?

Warning: Deception Ahead

As we will soon discover, each of Judah's sons' names (including his firstborn) will play directly into the narrative. But their names are not the only information we are given about their births.

> Reread Genesis 38:5. What else are we told in regard to the birth of Judah's third son?

Judah had been living in the land of Canaan, presumably in (or near) the city of Adullam. However, the writer inserts one additional detail: at the time of the birth of his third son, Shelah, Judah (and perhaps his family with him) was in Chezib. Stating the location of Shelah's birth is more than simply background information. Chezib was a small town not far from Adullam. The name of the town stems from the Hebrew root word *kazab*, which means *liar*, *lying*, or *deceiving*.[26]

As the story progresses, we will discover that the mention of this little town in the context of the birth of Judah's third son is fitting, as it foreshadows a deception to come. However, it is not the boy who deceives. As his name implies, Shelah remains silent throughout the entire narrative. Rather, the deception is hatched by his father, Judah.

> Think back on what you have read about Judah so far. What less-than-admirable character traits have you witnessed in his life up to this point?

The story's hint at future deception should not be surprising. After all, we have already seen Judah's willingness to lead his brothers to betray young Joseph, followed by slaughtering a goat to cover up their crime. Judah and his brothers then lie to their father about Joseph's fate, leaving their father to suffer in tormented grief.

Like Judah, for many of us, the first sin has a way of clearing the path for the next one. In time, it becomes easier and easier to justify our decisions to the point that we stop caring, or worse, we convince ourselves that our actions are not sinful at all.

PAUSE TO PONDER

> Reflect on the last statement, which is also printed in the margin. Think of a time when you saw this principle at work in your own life. What steps, if any, did you take in an effort to break the destructive cycle? What worked? What didn't? What can you do to guard yourself in the future?

Reread Genesis 38:6. What details are we given about Er's wife?

> The first sin clears the path for the next and then the next, making it easy to justify our decisions until we stop caring, or worse, deceive ourselves into thinking that our actions are not sinful at all.

It is curious that Scripture records even the name of the little town where Judah was when his third son was born, but it leaves us wanting more information about Tamar. After all, her actions are at the center of the chapter, as we will soon discover. Nevertheless, with a little bit of work, we can at least get a fairly good sense of how old Er and Tamar likely were when they married.

SUPPLEMENTAL READING

DO THE MATH . . . OR NOT

Okay, this one is for those of you who like math. We are going to calculate the age of Judah's son when he married Tamar. Before we begin, I'll admit it: I'm part nerd. I love math. I'm embarrassed to say that when I was around twelve years old, I sometimes made up math problems to see if I could solve them. I did this for fun. (I should get out more.)

But if the mention of math makes your upper lip curl, you're probably the kind of person I should have hung out with more. So here is your chance to escape. Feel free to skip ahead to the Math Overview section on page 91.

On the other hand, if you are a glutton for numerical punishment, here is how we calculate the age of Judah's son Er.

Marveling at God's Forbearance

Scripture Reference	Calculation	Years
Genesis 37:2, 41:46	How many years lapsed between Joseph being sold into slavery and him entering the service of the king of Egypt?	
Genesis 41:47-48, 53-54	How many years lapsed from the time Joseph entered the service of Egypt's king before the famine began? (How many years of plenty were there?)	
Genesis 42:1-4	Jacob's sons (including Judah) go to Egypt for the first time.	X
Genesis 43:1-3, 11, 15, 45:4-6	How many years lapsed from the start of the famine to the brothers' second visit to Egypt?	
	Total:	

So far, we know that roughly twenty-two years passed between the time Judah and his brothers sold Joseph into slavery and their second visit to Egypt during the famine.[27] Since the second visit took place only two years into the famine, we can estimate that the brothers' first visit to Egypt took place about a year earlier. Because Judah was among the brothers for the first visit as well as the second, this tells us that the events of Genesis 38 (occurring after Joseph was sold and before the brothers' first visit to Egypt) occurred over a period of roughly twenty-one years.

But we are not done. To calculate Er's age when he married Tamar, we need to factor in the events that took place in Genesis 38 before Er's birth and after his marriage to Tamar, since these events also would have taken place during the twenty-one years that span Genesis 38. Based on the narrative (which we will explore more fully in the weeks ahead), below is a reasonable estimate of the two time segments.

Scripture Reference	Calculation (Conservative Estimate)	Years
Genesis 38:1-3	Number of years between Joseph being sold into slavery and Judah's travel to Adullam, marriage, and birth of his son Er	1
Genesis 38:11, 42:1-4	Number of years between Er's marriage to Tamar and Judah's first trip to Egypt with his brothers	2
		Total: 3

21 years – 3 years = 18 years

Day Five / Week Two

Math Overview

Seeing that the events recorded in Genesis 38 occurred over a period of twenty-one years, based on the chronology, Judah's son Er would have been about eighteen years old when he married Tamar. While this was a young age for men to marry, it was not uncommon at that time. More often, however, men would wait to marry until they were established in a trade or occupation and thus prepared to provide for a family.

> Why might it be helpful to know how old Er was when he married Tamar? What insights might this information provide? (Note: there is no right or wrong answer to this question.)

There may be several reasons one might give for why knowing Er's age is helpful. The one that comes to my mind is that it helps us gain a closer estimation of Tamar's age, which, in turn, will deepen our understanding of how she may have experienced the events we are studying. Since Er would have been no more than eighteen or nineteen years old when he married Tamar, and since girls were nearly always younger than their husbands, Tamar was likely a girl when they married. She would have been perhaps thirteen or fourteen years old—the age shortly after a girl entered puberty—which was the common trigger for when girls were considered ready to marry.

.... YOUR TURN ....

> What was your life like when you were a young teen? What were your hopes and dreams? Or maybe you were trying to survive in a dysfunctional family. Looking back, how did those early years shape you? What one thing are you thankful for? Write a prayer of gratitude below.

Lesson Summary

What scripture, statement, or thought was most significant to you this week?*
Write it down, and then reword it into a prayer of response to God.

*Share your favorite takeaway with a friend or on social media using #TamarBibleStudy. At the end of each week, I will share a worship song that you may enjoy. This week's song is called "Lord, I Need You," by Matt Maher.

Notes

[1] William MacDonald, *Believer's Bible Commentary: Old and New Testaments*, ed. Arthur Farstad (Nashville: Thomas Nelson, 1995), 73.

[2] These four name descriptions are taken from the esv footnotes for Genesis 39:32–35.

[3] My friend, Kendra Burrows, has been a college instructor for more than twenty years. She applies both psychology and Scripture in her coaching practice to help people overcome negative thinking (KendraBurrows.com).

[4] The verb form is imperative in Hebrew, which means it is a command.

[5] For a better understanding of this practice and its consequences, see the Supplemental Reading, "Did Hagar Become Abraham's Wife?" in Week One of my Bible study Hagar.

[6] Matthew G. Easton, *Easton's Bible Dictionary* (New York: Harper & Brothers, 1893), s.v. "Mandrakes."

[7] Patricia L. Crawford and Mark Allan Powell, "Mandrake," in *The HarperCollins Bible Dictionary* (Revised and Updated), ed. Mark Allan Powell (New York: HarperCollins, 2011), 595; Easton, "Mandrakes."

[8] Steven P. Carpenter, *The Story of Joseph and Judah: A Teacher's Narrative and Structural Commentary on Genesis 37–50* (Fort Lauderdale, FL: St. Andrews House, 2010), 9.

[9] The Ishmaelites (descendants of Abraham through Sarah's slave Hagar) and the Midianites (descendants of Abraham through his second wife Keturah) are at times loosely associated with each other due to their shared identity as being "people of the East" (Gen. 25:6).

[10] Julia Jones, *Face2Face with Tamar, Bathsheba, and Tamar: Encountering Three Women with Messed-Up Lives*, ed. Simon J. Robinson, Face2Face Series (Leominster, UK: Day One Publications, 2008), 9.

[11] Nahum M. Sarna, *The JPS Torah Commentary: Genesis* (Philadelphia: Jewish Publication Society, 1989), 262.

[12] The plural reference to daughters in Genesis 37:35 likely included his daughters-in-law.

[13] Carpenter, *The Story of Joseph and Judah*, 16.

[14] I am quoting from the ESV Bible. Some English translations state: "stayed with," "settled near," or "visited a certain."

[15] John D. Currid, *A Study Commentary on Genesis: Genesis 25:19–50:26*, vol. 2 (Darlington, UK: 2003), 207.

[16] James Strong, *A Concise Dictionary of the Words in the Greek Testament and The Hebrew Bible* (Bellingham, WA: Logos Bible Software, 2009), 114; Stelman Smith and Judson Cornwall, The Exhaustive Dictionary of Bible Names (North Brunswick, NJ: Bridge-Logos, 1998), 225.

[17] Yigal Tzadka, Orly Kihaly, and David Herman, eds., *Choice Words from the Story of Judah and Tamar* (Jerusalem: Good Times Ltd., n.d.), 10.

[18] Other relevant Old Testament passages include Joshua 23:11–13, Ezra 9:1–2, and Nehemiah 13:27, to name a few.

[19] Carpenter, *The Story of Joseph and Judah*, 20.

[20] Simply because two spouses remain together does not mean the marriage is working or healthy.

[21] If you or someone you care about has suffered the heartache of a past abortion, I invite you to consider my Bible study *Worthy of Love: A Journey of Hope and Healing after Abortion*, based on my own personal story.

[22] David D. Pettus, "Tamar, Daughter-in-Law of Judah," in *The Lexham Bible Dictionary*, ed. John D. Barry et al. (Bellingham, WA: Lexham Press, 2016).

[23] A few include Gary H. Oller, "Tamar (Person)," in *The Anchor Yale Bible Dictionary*, ed. David Noel Freedman (New York: Doubleday, 1992), 315; Phyllis A. Bird and Mark Allan Powell, "Tamar," in *The HarperCollins Bible Dictionary (Revised and Updated)*, ed. Mark Allan Powell (New York: HarperCollins, 2011), 1,009; David D. Pettus, "Tamar, Daughter-in-Law of Judah," in Lexham Bible Dictionary, ed. John D. Barry et al. (Bellingham, WA: Lexham Press, 2016).

[24] J. D. Douglas, "Onan," in *New Bible Dictionary*, ed. D. R. W. Wood et al. (Downers Grove, IL: InterVarsity Press, 1996), 848.

[25] Robert L. Thomas, *New American Standard Hebrew-Aramaic and Greek Dictionaries: Updated Edition* (Anaheim: Foundation Publications, Inc., 1998).

[26] Chad Brand et al., eds., *Holman Illustrated Bible Dictionary* (Nashville: Holman Bible Publishers, 2003), s.v. "Chezib."

[27] Further explanation concerning the list of persons who came with Jacob to Egypt in Genesis 46:12 will be provided when we examine the passage in Week Six.

NOTES

NOTES

NOTES

LESSONS FROM

FLOOD

WEEK THREE

THIS WEEK, WE WILL DISCOVER THAT TAMAR'S MARRIAGE is as far from idyllic as one can get. No sooner does the young girl join Judah's family than a flood of tragedy erupts, beginning with her husband. Apart from his name and being Judah's firstborn son, Scripture records merely one detail about the man: he was "wicked in the sight of the LORD" (Gen. 38:7), words that precisely mirror God's judgment fourteen generations earlier in the days of Noah.

DAY ONE
When Your Dream Becomes a Nightmare

Tamar lived in a society where girls were married young and expected to begin producing children shortly thereafter. As if that were not difficult enough, they would have no say in who their father chose to be their husband. Their father's decisions often revolved around financial or other benefits the marriage would bring to the family. In effect, marriages were little more than business arrangements.

Nevertheless, although the era and culture may be vastly different from ours, there are some things about marriage that are not bound by time or place, such as a young bride's hopes and dreams—and fears. Imagine that you are young Tamar and you learn that someone has come to speak to your father about your

betrothal. You don't know any details at this point or even who it was that came to present the marriage proposal to your father.

If you are Tamar, what questions might be going through your mind? List as many as you can think of.

How about your emotions? What feelings might you be experiencing at this point?

Then it happens. Your father asks to see you. He announces that you will marry the son of Judah, the Hebrew. Your mind races. You've heard of these Hebrews, how they worship just one god—a strange one at that, for He is invisible. Apart from that, you know nothing about this Judah or his son. Well, that's not true. You are informed that they live in Adullam,[1] which is about a two-hour walk from where your family lives.[2] Not far, you console yourself. But you can't help but wonder, What will my future be like? Will my husband love me? How many children will we have? What's it like in Adullam? Will I miss my family? Will they miss me? Is my mother-in-law kind? Will she like me? Will I make new friends?

Hundreds of thoughts would be going through young Tamar's mind. None, however, could prepare her for what happens next.

> "When I am afraid, I put my trust in you." —Psalm 56:3

PAUSE TO PONDER

How can you relate to Tamar? Where in your life right now are you (or someone you love) struggling with an unknown? In what way(s) do you see God currently at work in this situation? Make a list of the things you can give God praise for. If you do not yet see God at work in this situation, ask Him to reveal whether there is anything you need to confess or surrender to Him. Then ask God to help you see how He might be using the situation for good.

Day One / Week Three

Read Genesis 38:6-7 (verse 6 is a review). Describe what happens and why.

Before we dive into these events in more detail, there is one observation that I want to point out. It concerns the Hebrew word translated *wicked* and how that relates to the name of Judah's firstborn son. Let's take a look.

In the space below, trace the Hebrew word meaning *wicked* by using a pen or pencil. Next to that, trace the Hebrew name *Er*.

Trace the word *wicked* in Hebrew:	Trace the name *Er* in Hebrew:
רע	ער

Compare the Hebrew text for both words; what observations can you make?

Fun fact: Ancient Hebrew was originally written in consonants. Vowels (appearing as small dots and dashes) were added later.

Changing Directions

In Hebrew, Er's name is spelled *ayin-resh*; spelled backward, it becomes *resh-ayin*. In Hebrew, *resh-ayin* spells *wicked* or *evil*[3] (these are the same in Hebrew). Not only does Scripture describe Er as wicked (and in case we missed it, Scripture repeats this fact in 1 Chronicles 2:3), but tomorrow we'll see there is another connection in the Bible relating to Er's name. However, I want to add a note of caution. When studying Scripture, taking a word or name and looking at it spelled backward should be done with tremendous discretion; I would not advise it unless there are other compelling reasons that suggest a connection is intended by the writer, which is the case here, as we will see tomorrow. While we may not know the meaning of Er's name, there is more going on with his name than meets the eye.

When Scripture Is Silent

After we read about Judah's wife and the birth of their three sons in Genesis 38:1–5, the writer seems in a hurry to move into the next series of events in the story. A considerable chunk of time has passed between verses 5 and 6. Er has grown up, and Judah decides he is ready to marry. The next thing we read is that

Lessons from God's Flood

Judah takes a wife for his firstborn, and then something shocking happens: "But Er, Judah's firstborn, was wicked in the sight of the Lord, and the Lord put him to death" (v. 7).

If this were the opening line of a novel, it would be quite the attention-getter, except for one thing: Scripture never tells us what Er did. What was so evil that God would immediately strike the man dead? Let's be honest; it's a frustrating omission, wouldn't you say? While we cannot be entirely certain when Scripture is silent, I do believe there are some clues that can help us formulate a reason for God's severe judgment.

In our English translations of the Old Testament, the words *evil* and *wicked* (and other variations, such as *wickedness*) stem from the same root Hebrew word, *ra*. The word is first introduced at the beginning of Genesis, where we read about the "tree of the knowledge of good and evil" (Gen. 2:9, 2:17, 3:5, 3:22). From there, the word appears frequently throughout the Old Testament. However, up to this point in the book of Genesis, the word appears several times in direct relation to God's judgment on sin leading to death.

> Reread Genesis 6:2, 6:5, and 6:11. What type of wickedness provoked God's anger prior to the worldwide flood? Circle all that apply.
>
> violence   idolatry   sexual sin   robbing the poor
>
> Read Genesis 19:1-7 and 19:24-25, which briefly outline God's judgment on the cities of Sodom and Gomorrah. What type of wickedness were the men of the city instigating? (Optional: see also 2 Peter 2:7.) Circle all that apply.
>
> violence   idolatry   sexual sin   robbing the poor
>
> Consider humanity's wickedness in Noah's day and in the days of Sodom and Gomorrah. What does God's response to their wickedness reveal about His character?

The Use of Words

After the references to "the tree of knowledge of good and evil" in the garden of Eden (Gen. 2:9, 2:17; as well as "knowing good and evil" in general—Gen. 3:5, 3:22), the next appearance of the word *wicked* (or *evil*) occurs in Genesis 6–8 with God's judgment on sin (sexual sin is specifically mentioned, although there

Day One / Week Three

were others). Genesis 6:5 tells us that "every intention of the thoughts of [man's] heart was only evil continually." That's a tragic pronouncement. In the end, God's judgment resulted in the destruction of the entire human race save Noah and his family (Gen. 6:7-8, 7:23). However, it would only be a matter of time before the seed of wickedness in man's heart would once again take root. Several chapters later, the issue of wickedness resurfaces, this time in the story of Sodom and Gomorrah (Gen. 13:13, 18:23, 18:25, 19:7). Here again, sexual sin is highlighted, though there were others (see Ezekiel 16:49). After the destruction of those cities, a pronouncement of God's judgment on sin leading to death does not resurface until we come to Genesis 38.

First it was God's judgment on evil in the days of Noah. Then it was God's judgment on the evil of the men in the cities of Sodom and Gomorrah. In both cases, sexual sin was prominent and, in both cases, judgment resulted in death. The events surrounding the flood and the destruction of Sodom and Gomorrah, followed by God's death sentence on Er for his wickedness, suggests that Er's sin may have been sexual in nature. Several factors add further weight to this hypothesis.

First, Scripture describes Er himself—rather than a specific behavior—as wicked. There is only one other place in the book of Genesis where persons are described in this exact same manner.

Write Genesis 13:13.

> "The eyes of the LORD are toward the righteous and his ears toward their cry. The face of the LORD is against those who do evil, to cut off the memory of them from the earth." —Psalm 34:15-16

Apart from the description of Er in Genesis 38:7, Genesis 13:13 is the only other place in Genesis where *wicked* is used to describe a person (or in this case, a group of people). The *Lexham Bible Dictionary* considers the connection noteworthy: "Though the narrator [of Genesis] does not specify the nature of Er's evil, this word [*wicked*] also describes the doomed men of Sodom in Genesis 13:13."[4] In other words, the parallel wording suggests that the judgment may relate to sexual behavior in both cases.

Second, we do not need to look far in order to trace the terrible sexual ethic modeled within his own family. From his grandfather Jacob taking not only two wives but also adding to that two concubines (Gen. chapters 29 and 30) to his father Judah who merely looks at a woman and decides to take her for himself (Gen. 38:2). In fact, Judah's impulsive sexual appetite will later become even more apparent. With such a heritage as this, perhaps it should not be surprising that the heart of Er would reflect that of his father's—even worse.

Lessons from God's Flood

Finally, there is one last element of the story that adds even more weight to the idea that Er's sin was sexual in nature.

When did God's judgment on Er occur? Before or after he married Tamar? Circle your response.

    before   after

- If Er was wicked, why do you suppose God did not strike him dead prior to him getting married? What correlation might there be between the timing of God's judgment and Er's marriage?

> "The LORD saw that the wickedness of man was great in the earth, and that every intention of the thoughts of his heart was only evil continually."
> —Genesis 6:5

While we cannot be entirely certain as to what led God to strike Tamar's husband dead, a study of the text, along with his family history, suggests that it may have been related to sexual sin. The fact that God's judgment occurs immediately after Er's marriage, not before, suggests that the circumstances of marriage itself (that is, sexual union) played a part.

What do the following scriptures reveal about God's ideal for marriage?

Hebrews 13:4

Colossians 3:19

Compare the attitudes, values, and behaviors concerning marriage and sexuality in our world today with those in Noah's day and in the days of Sodom and Gomorrah. Would you say they are similar or different or somewhere in between? Mark an X on the line below.

_____
similar   different

Consider the attitudes, values, and behaviors concerning marriage and sexuality among people throughout human history up through today. How do they compare with God's design? Mark an X on the line below.

_____
similar   different

Day One / Week Three

What conclusions can you draw?

PAUSE TO PONDER

> (Optional: read Ephesians 5:3–5 and Ephesians 5:11–12.) Consider your personal attitudes, values, and behaviors concerning marriage and sexuality. How do they currently line up with God's design? Is there an area in which, looking back, you see that you have come closer to reaching God's ideal? Is there an area in which you still fall short? What steps will you take to move closer to God's design?

A Tragic Beginning

Try to put yourself in Tamar's sandals. How might the events recorded in Genesis 38:7 affect you? What might be going through your mind and heart?

Here you are: a young bride taken into a strange home of one man, three teenage boys—one of whom is your husband—and a mother-in-law. You quickly discover, perhaps on your wedding night, that your husband is not at all as you had hoped and dreamed. In fact, he is downright evil. You're trapped. You have no rights. You might even pray to your gods, the only ones you've ever known. Maybe you even send up a prayer to Judah's God—it certainly couldn't hurt. Then suddenly, boom! Your husband is dead. If you were frantic before, that was nothing compared to this. Your mind races. "What's going to happen next? Will I be punished? Am I with child? Will I be sent away? Will my family take me back?"

Tamar has no answers; all she knows at this point is that her husband is dead.

YOUR TURN

Do not be anxious about anything, but in everything by prayer and supplication with thanksgiving let your requests be made known to God. And the peace of God, which surpasses all understanding, will guard your hearts and your minds in Christ Jesus.

Philippians 4:6–7

Think back on the past two weeks. List two or three things you have been most anxious about.

Consider Philippians 4:6-7, which is printed on the prior page. What does God promise in His Word when you choose to bring your worries to Him in prayer?

What worry will you bring to God in prayer this week?

Write a prayer of commitment below.

DAY TWO
Witnessing God's Intervention on Your Behalf

We finally get our first glimpse into the life of Tamar—let's be honest, it's not looking bright. In two verses, she is married, likely mistreated in some way, and abruptly widowed. However, while these events are sobering—and this is only the beginning of Tamar's story—right from the start we are given a glimmer of hope because Tamar is not the only one who suddenly comes onto the scene.

> Glance back through the events in Genesis 37:1-36. How many times does the name of the Lord appear in the story of Judah (and his brothers') betrayal and deception?

Glance back through the events in Genesis 38:1-5. How many times does the name of the Lord appear within the context of Judah leaving his family, marrying a Canaanite, and fathering three sons?

When does the name of the Lord reenter the narrative? What is happening in Genesis 38:6-7? List each person in the passage and how they were involved.

_____:

_____:

_____:

_____:

Whether or not Er's wickedness involved direct abuse of his young bride in some way, what might God's sudden appearance in the narrative at this point in time suggest about God's concern for Tamar?

> "When I look at your heavens, the work of your fingers ... what is man that you are mindful of him, and the son of man that you care for him?"
> —Psalm 8:3-4

PAUSE TO PONDER

When did you first become aware of God's presence in *your* life story? What difference has it made? What one thing are you most thankful for?

What's in a Name?

I still remember the first time I learned the meaning of my name. My parents had recently divorced, and my mother, brother, and I moved into a rent-controlled

apartment in the Queens borough of New York City. My family had already moved several times prior (from Manhattan's Lower East Side to the outskirts of Las Vegas to Morocco [where my father was born] and then back to New York). Talk about culture shock! For a twelve-year-old, starting over at a new school where I knew no one was hard enough. Add to that my strange accent and peculiar name—which no one could pronounce, let alone remember—it made for some hard days.

One evening, after I was ridiculed at school that day because of my unusual name, my mother asked if something was wrong. I told her what was happening and that I wished I had a "normal" name. She immediately reassured me. "Why? Your name is beautiful! It means *singing birds*." The next day, when the teasing began, I proudly announced the meaning of my name: "It means *singing birds*." "More like screeching owls!" a boy snapped back.

I eventually came to terms with my name. Today, I have come to embrace it. It even has some benefits: it's easy to find me on social media, and if you can spell my name, you can find me! Nevertheless, until God called me to serve Him through writing and speaking, I always thought the meaning of my name was ironic considering the fact that I have no singing ability. However, I later discovered that my name also means *beautiful voice*. As a teacher, that I can live with, as long as I don't have to sing in public.

Let's pause here for a moment to appreciate how much we have learned up to this point. To help give us a framework for the rest of today's lesson, we will do a quick review of the events and discoveries we have explored so far.

> How is the name of Judah's firstborn son connected to the description of him as being "wicked" in Genesis 38:7? (Hint: glance back at page 99.)

> In the book of Genesis, after we read about the garden of Eden and before we come to the story of Tamar in Genesis 38, the Hebrew word for *wicked* (or *evil*) appears in association with two specific events. What are they? (Hint: glance back at Genesis 6 and 19.)
>
> 1.
>
> 2.

"Not to us, O LORD, not to us, but to your name give glory, for the sake of your steadfast love and your faithfulness!" —Psalm 115:1

Day Two / Week Three

What do these two events have in common?

Consider what we have learned so far. First, Scripture describes Er as wicked; other than his name and being Judah's firstborn son, these are the only things the Bible reveals about him. Then, we uncovered the curious wordplay on his name with the Hebrew word for *wicked*. Next, we saw that the word *wicked* (or *evil*) appears earlier in Genesis in direct relation to humanity's corrupt sexual behavior—not once, but twice! Not only that, but in both episodes, their wickedness leads to God's judgment and a sentence of death. Based on these facts, there is a strong indication that Er's wicked behavior was sexual in nature. However, there is something else in the Genesis narrative that adds even more weight to this hypothesis. Let's take a look.

Carefully examine Genesis 6:2–7 and 38:2–7, which are printed below. Read the passages two times (at least once out loud). Then, using different types of marks, such as circles, boxes, or brackets (or different-color highlighters), identify pairs of keywords, phrases, or concepts that appear in both passages. I marked one pair for you with bold type.

> The sons of God **saw that the daughters** of man were attractive. And they took as their wives any they chose. . . . the sons of God came in to the daughters of man and they bore children to them. . . . The Lord saw that the wickedness of man was great in the earth, and that every intention of the thoughts of his heart was only evil continually. . . . So the Lord said, "I will blot out man whom I have created from the face of the land." (Gen. 6:2–7, selected)

> There Judah **saw the daughter** of a certain Canaanite whose name was Shua. He took her and went in to her, and she conceived and bore a son . . . . And Judah took a wife for Er his firstborn, and her name was Tamar. But Er, Judah's firstborn, was wicked in the sight of the Lord, and the Lord put him to death. (Gen. 38:2–7, selected)

I trust that you found several parallels between the passages. These parallels strongly suggest that the passages are related in some way. And yet, as the dear women in my Bible study group love to say, "But wait! There's more!"

Reread Genesis 6:8 in your Bible. What are we told about Noah?

Lessons from God's Flood

In the space below, trace the Hebrew word *favor* by using a pen or pencil. Next to that, trace the Hebrew name *Noah*.

Trace the word *favor* in Hebrew:	Trace the name *Noah* in Hebrew:
חן	נח

Compare the Hebrew text for both words; what observations can you make? (Note: the Hebrew letters ן and נ are two forms of the same letter.)

In Hebrew, Noah's name is spelled *nun-het*; spelled backward, it becomes *het-nun*.[5] In Hebrew, *het-nun* spells *favor*.[6] Noah's name reversed spells *favor*. In English, *favor* may seem a somewhat benign term. In Scripture, however, especially throughout the Genesis narrative, the word is used as a remarkable portrayal of relationship, as people seek or even beg for favor with one another and with God.[7] When we consider the other parallels between the narratives and the fact that the favored one is saved from God's wrath whereas the wicked one is destroyed by it, we can see that this reverse wordplay on the names of Noah and Er is no coincidence. If we had a strong indication that Er's wicked behavior was sexual in nature before, these additional connections leave little doubt. There is a reason why this is so important. Remember what God is after: He is bringing a Savior into the world, and He chose the family line of Abraham through whom the Savior would come. While every human being falls short because of sin, it seems that God was unwilling to bless Er's union to Tamar.

Earlier, you had an opportunity to identify parallels between the narratives when I asked you to mark pairs of keywords, passages, or concepts that appear in both passages. The following exercise will help uncover any you might have missed.

For the following pairs of brief excerpts taken from Genesis 6:2–7 and 38:2–7, fill in the blanks with the appropriate word or phrase based on the passages. I completed the first lines for you.

From Genesis 6:2–7

the sons of God saw that the daughters of man

they _____ wives . . . and _____ children to them

Day Two / Week Three

The Lord _____ that the _____ of man was great

So the Lord said, "I will _____ man..."

From Genesis 38:2-7

Judah saw the daughter of a certain

He _____ her and... she _____ a son

Er was _____ in the _____ of the Lord and the Lord put him

to _____

Now, go back to the original exercise, and mark any parallels you previously missed.

Just a few verses into Tamar's story, and we are suddenly transported back to the events leading up to the flood. Who knew? Well, God knew, and when we take the time to dig deeply into His Word, we will find a wonderful treasure trove that breathes new life into passages we may have read many times before.

................................YOUR TURN..................................

Now that we have a panoramic view of the backdrop in which Tamar's story appears within God's grand redemptive plan, this week we will start zooming in on the details.

I have been a bookworm all my life (attested to by the stack of "reader of the year" awards my mother collected when I was a child). I have always loved to read, and I still do. When it comes to reading stories (whether fiction or nonfiction), I have discovered that readers fall into essentially one of two camps: those who enjoy reading a story as it unfolds, from beginning to end, and those who, the moment they get their hands on a new book, jump to the last pages and read the ending first.

Which one are you? Circle one.

    read the ending last   read the ending first

I confess that I fall into the first camp, which makes what I am about to propose contrary to my reading style. However, because the story of Tamar is somewhat complex, having an overview of the full story will provide a helpful framework as we move forward.

> "The eyes of the Lord are in every place, keeping watch on the evil and the good." —Proverbs 15:3

Today or sometime this week, read all of Genesis 38 (if you have already done so, then you are ahead of the game!).

Day Three
When You Thought It Couldn't Get Any Worse

*But our citizenship is in heaven,
and from it we await a Savior, the Lord Jesus Christ.*

Philippians 3:20

> "The memory of the righteous is a blessing, but the name of the wicked will rot."
>
> —Proverbs 10:7

Because of my unusual name, I am often asked about my family background and nationality. I was born in the ethnic melting pot of Manhattan's Lower East Side, the first child of my immigrant parents. My father came to the United States from Morocco, and my mother came from Latvia. In time, I came to have three parents (stepdad makes three), and, together, they could not have made a more diverse religious mix, coming from Muslim, Lutheran, and Jewish homes. While I love my family heritage, I am forever thankful that through Jesus Christ my Lord, my true "citizenship is in heaven" (Phil. 3:20).

When we first encounter Tamar in Scripture, we are not told her nationality, ancestry, or any other information that we might expect to be recorded. Since we later learn that Tamar's father was still living nearby, it seems that his name and nationality are irrelevant. But Tamar's name *is* recorded—God chose to include her name in His holy Word for a reason. It is not the ancestry Tamar was born into that is relevant; instead, it is the ancestry that would be born *out* from her, but I'm getting ahead of myself.

The Right Choice for the Wrong Reasons

Just as God chose to invite Tamar into His story, Judah also had reasons for choosing Tamar, in this case, for his son. Scripture never mentions what Tamar looked like. But as we have discovered, the narrative in the beginning of Genesis 38 strongly parallels events recorded in Genesis 6. There, we read in verse 2 that "the sons of God saw that the daughters of man were attractive . . . they took as their wives any they chose." Let's pause here for a moment to examine where else this combination of "saw" and "took" takes place in Genesis to see what we can discover.

For each passage below, record who the subject is, what the person(s) "saw" and "took" (or seized), and what the motivation was. I completed two for you.

Reference	Who?	"Saw" and "took" (seized) what?	What was the motivation?
Genesis 3:1-6			
Genesis 6:1-2	Sons of God	Daughters of man	They were attractive; to marry/sleep with them
Genesis 12:14-19			
Genesis 34:1-4			
Genesis 38:1-2	Judah	Daughter of a Canaanite	He saw her; to marry/sleep with her
2 Samuel 11:2-4			

Looking at the table, compare and contrast all the passages after Genesis 3 (the Fall); what similarities do you notice?

 How does Genesis 3:1-6 shed light on the other passages?

All the passages use the same Hebrew verb combination, typically translated *saw* and *took* (or *seized* in Genesis 34:2).[8] We see it first in the garden of Eden where Eve sees and takes the forbidden fruit. "Later on, the combination is used to describe lust, especially sexual lust with this residual idea of forbidden fruit."[9] These parallels, coupled with Judah's earlier choice to reject God's covenant plan by *taking* (marrying) a Canaanite because he *saw* her, suggests that at this point in Judah's life, it is his emotions and appetites—and likely that of his son as well—that are at the heart of his choices.[10]

Concerning Judah's marriage to Shua's daughter, one commentary author writes, "Judah is a son of God [that is, he is part of God's covenant family] who here has decided to follow his own lust and abandon the restrictions of the covenant into which he was born. And his apostasy is so great that the author wants us to think of the wickedness that caused the flood."[11] The fact that the author of Genesis is describing Judah's behavior in the shadow of God's wrath in Genesis 6

Lessons from God's Flood

is meant to give us a glimpse into Judah's heart, in which lust seems to have taken root and ripened to full measure within his half-Canaanite son.

While we do not know how long Tamar's marriage to Er lasted, the rapid succession of events seems to indicate that God's judgment on Er came swiftly. Right from the start, we see evidence of God's mercy for Tamar. He looked down from heaven and saw Er's wickedness and Tamar's helplessness. He did not have to step in, but He did.

> ### PAUSE TO PONDER
>
> Think of a time when God intervened when you suffered. How did God step in? What impact did it have on your relationship with God? If you cannot think of a time when God intervened on your behalf, take some time over the next few days and ask God to reveal how He has intervened for you in the past. Come back and record what He reveals.

Second Chances

Read Genesis 38:8. Describe what happens next.

Why do you suppose Judah does not place any blame on Tamar or attempt to get rid of her? List as many possibilities as you can think of.

Imagine you are Tamar—what options do you have? To whom can you turn?

Judah gives Tamar to his second-born son because a child had not been conceived through Er. Judah places no blame on Tamar for either Er's demise or the fact that a child had not been conceived. Had Judah wanted to get rid of her, here was his chance. It would have been easy for him to send her away (after all, he didn't think twice about selling his own brother). As for Tamar, her only viable option, other than remain, would be to try to return home.

However, in that society, a daughter-in-law was essentially purchased by the family. Even if Tamar tried to return home, a childless widow would be considered a burden on her family. One commentary author goes so far as to say that such a woman was "considered worthless in that culture."[12]

Yet, in spite of all that Tamar has endured to this point:

- Scripture never mentions that Tamar tried to run away.
- Judah finds no fault in Tamar.
- Judah does not falsely accuse Tamar in an attempt to get rid of her.

What might the above truths suggest about Tamar's character?

Now imagine being Tamar; what might you be thinking or feeling at this point?

Judah was employing a practice called levirate marriage. The *Lexham Bible Dictionary* sums it up well: "It was the duty of the nearest male relative of a deceased man to marry the childless widow and to father her children. Her firstborn son would then be acknowledged as the son of her deceased husband and would inherit his property. This practice is known as levirate marriage (from 'levir,' Latin for 'husband's brother')."[13]

Although God's laws had not been written yet, the practice of levirate marriage was common at that time. In fact, "many ancient Near Eastern societies practiced levirate marriage, including Babylon, Assyria, the Hittites. . . . The custom was also present in parts of modern Africa and Asia."[14]

Lessons from God's Flood

Read Deuteronomy 25:5-6. What is the purpose of this law? List all the outcomes that result when the law is practiced.

Read Deuteronomy 25:7-9. Does the brother of the deceased husband have a choice in whether to marry his brother's widow? What are the consequences if he refuses?

Read Genesis 38:9.

~ Why do you think Onan was unwilling to produce offspring that would legally be counted as the offspring of Er? (Hint: What did Onan have to lose? See also Deut. 21:17.)

A Double Portion of Suffering

Onan, who would have been no more than seventeen years old, was Judah's second-born son. If Er had died prior to marrying Tamar, Onan would have legally inherited a much larger portion of Judah's estate. However, if Er were to have a legal heir, then that son would receive Er's inheritance. It seems that Judah's propensity toward greed had passed on to his son. But Onan's greed involved more than wealth and possessions.

In what manner did Onan refuse to produce an heir for his brother? Circle one.

He refused to marry Tamar.

He refused to sleep with Tamar.

He refused to impregnate Tamar.

Carefully reread Genesis 38:9. Is Onan's behavior a one-time occurrence?

Yes   No

What does this reveal about Onan's character? ~

How does Onan betray each person listed below?

Judah:

Er:

Tamar:

God: (Hint: see Rom. 2:12–16)

The purpose of levirate marriage was twofold: first, to produce a child for the deceased brother (or relative), thereby propagating his memory and ensuring his family line would not die with him (which was of utmost importance at that time); second, it would protect the childless widow from being married outside the family and having to sell herself in order to provide for her daily needs[15] or needing to pay off any debt that may have been attached to her husband or his property.[16]

Levirate marriage was common at the time, as attested to by the way Judah speaks to his son Onan. In Genesis 38:8, each of the three verbs quoted of Judah are in the imperative verb form in Hebrew, which means that they are commands: "go in to" (have intercourse), "perform the duty of a brother-in-law" (marry, as in levirate marriage), and "raise up offspring for your brother." However, rather than refusing to marry Tamar (which he could have done) and risk losing his father's favor and incurring public shame, Onan instead secretly treats Tamar like a prostitute. He shows no concern for her feelings and has no intention of giving her a child but freely uses her for sex. His actions are done repeatedly as attested to by the words in Genesis 38:9, "whenever he went."

In ancient society, having children, especially sons, was not only considered a woman's highest honor, it was also a means for her survival. Tamar would have wanted to conceive a son as much as Judah hoped she would, perhaps even more. Imagine Tamar's daily life in her in-laws' home and new community. Picture her going about her household duties, serving her mother-in-law, fetching water from the community well, and serving and eating dinner with her new family.

In addition to Onan's selfish mistreatment, list all the other ways Tamar may have been suffering.

Lessons from God's Flood

Which manner of Tamar's suffering is most heartbreaking to you? Why?

From the outside, Onan gives the impression to Judah, his family, and the community that he is faithfully fulfilling his father's wishes and honoring his deceased brother. All the while, he is doing nothing more than selfishly indulging his sexual appetite. Meanwhile, Tamar, who is, at most, fourteen or fifteen years old, is trapped in his deception.

.........................YOUR TURN.........................

I lift up my eyes to the hills. From where does my help come? My help comes from the Lord, who made heaven and earth.

Psalm 121:1–2

Have you ever experienced a time when you suffered but felt you had no one to turn to? In what way(s) can you relate to Tamar?

Think back to the time before you knew God (or, if you were young when you became a Christian, think of the early years in your life as a believer). When you encountered difficult circumstances, to whom did you instinctively turn first for help? Why?

When you encounter difficult circumstances now, to whom do you instinctively turn first for help? Is your answer different from the previous one? Why or why not?

Read Psalm 121:1-2 above. Why should we go to God first when we are in need? What difference does it make?

Day Three / Week Three

Day Four
Dysfunction Is a Family Affair

Last week, I shared briefly about how my marriage came to an end. Today, I would like to share a bit more with you about how the relationship started. Actually, "like" to share is not entirely true—it's never easy to share these kinds of stories, but I suspect I'm not the only one who can relate in some way to Tamar and the heartache of abuse, mistreatment, or dysfunctional relationships.

I met my former husband a few weeks before my eighteenth birthday; he was twenty-six. When I consider all the years of hiding the truth, perhaps the greatest misery was feeling that I was alone and had nowhere to turn. Looking back, I believe part of it was my pride—I was too ashamed to admit what a terrible mistake I had made.

During the first year of our relationship, there were several incidents of physical abuse. After the first time it happened, I left him, only to be called repeatedly by a close member of his family who begged me to go back because he was threatening to kill himself. Sadly, I went back—a tragic testimony of our codependent relationship.

I'll never forget one evening in particular. He was sitting next to me at the kitchen table where we were having dinner with his family. At the end of the meal, I raised my arms behind my head to stretch. My shirt sleeves fell from my wrists to my elbows, revealing a large purple bruise on my forearm. I had momentarily forgotten it was there until my husband reached over and quietly lowered my arm. Shamed into silence, I knew several at the table had seen it, but no one said a word.

As time went on, the abuse shifted to mostly verbal assaults, threats, and violent outbursts—always coupled with him threatening to kill himself if I left him. Because I believed him, I stayed. Several more years went by. Then, one day, weary of the emotional and mental toll of our relationship, I found the courage to reach out for help. I wrote a note to a member of my husband's family who seemed especially religious. "Surely this time they will help me," I reasoned. In the note, I explained what was happening and asked for help. The next time we visited their home, I placed the note where I believed it would be safe and would be found. The note was never acknowledged.

Ten more years went by.

Hiding behind a Mask

When the economy suffered a downturn, my husband and I moved from New York to California. It didn't take long before we found new jobs, settled into an

apartment, and began to make new friends. Among these new friends was a Christian couple who invited us to a weekly Bible study led by a pastor and his wife. Although I had not been raised in the church and did not believe in God, in only six months, both my husband and I had made a profession of faith, been baptized, and started attending church. I was thrilled to discover there was a God who loved me. However, I still had an unhealthy marriage. My husband was an alcoholic and prone to fits of rage, and I suffered from codependency and depression.

One day, the pastor of the small church we were attending invited us to his home in an effort to help us grow in our new faith. As we were driving to his house, my husband started an argument. By the time we parked in front of the house, I was on the verge of tears. This invited more threats; the last thing my husband wanted was for someone to know how he was treating me, especially a pastor. Before we stepped out of the car, I did what I had mastered over the years: I put on a fake smile and hid behind my mask. After we entered the pastor's home and exchanged pleasantries, we sat down together in the living room. Seated across from us, the pastor took one look at me and immediately fixed his attention on my husband.

"So, how are you treating your wife?"

I was stunned. "He knows!" my heart cried out. Though I spoke not a word, nor let a tear fall from my eyes, God gave that pastor discernment as to what was happening *behind the seen*. For the first time in that fourteen-year relationship, I had hope.

"You are my hiding place and my shield; I hope in your word." —Psalm 119:114

PAUSE TO PONDER

> Looking back on your life as an adult, did you ever feel compelled to "hide behind a mask"—perhaps in a relationship, at work or school, or even at church? Did you share your struggle with anyone? If so, what was the result? How might hiding behind a mask keep you from experiencing God's best?

Strike Two

Let's do a quick review. Tamar, a young bride of perhaps thirteen or fourteen years old, is taken into Judah's home and married to his wicked son, Er. After God strikes Er dead for his wickedness, Tamar is given to Judah's second born, Onan, in order to produce a legal heir for the deceased brother. Onan ignores his father's wishes and even spits in the face of common decency by treating young Tamar as he might treat a prostitute.

How likely were Tamar's chances that things would improve without God's intervention? Who could she turn to for help?

Read Genesis 38:9-10 (verse 9 is a review).

How did God intervene?

Do you find God's judgment extreme? Surprising? Share your thoughts.

To God, Onan's behavior and mistreatment of Tamar is no small matter. Although the law had not yet been written, the practice of levirate marriage was already well established. One commentator explains that Onan, in refusing to fulfill his levirate obligation, "placed his sexual relationship with his sister-in-law in the category of incest—a capital offense"[17] (Lev. 18:6, 16; 20:21).

But Onan's sin had consequences even beyond that. Little did he know that his father would one day be placed in the direct lineage of Jesus Christ. As such, Onan's refusal to give Tamar a child "affected the genealogy by which Christ would inherit legal right to the throne of David."[18] God considers Onan's behavior so abominable that He takes his life. His judgment is swift and complete.[19]

PAUSE TO PONDER

In what way(s) have you personally experienced God's intervention at a time when you were helpless to change your situation?

Tamar's second husband is now dead. Describe the affect this may have had on:

Tamar:

Lessons from God's Flood

Judah:

Shelah (who was likely a young teen):

Even if both sons' deaths were attributed to accidents or natural, albeit sudden, causes, what suspicions might have arisen among friends and neighbors in response to these events?

 How might these suspicions have contributed to the family's grief?

Turning a Blind Eye

Try to picture the distress Judah and his wife were experiencing, not only their grief in having to bury two young sons but that neither son left behind any children. We can only imagine what may have been going through the minds of their friends and neighbors.

To be honest, when I consider the events in the story, I can't help but scratch my head. Did Judah have no idea what was going on under his own roof? Did he have no clue of the moral degeneracy of his two oldest sons? Not just one son is struck dead, but two? Did Judah not see God's hand of judgment in any of this?

Sadly, whether due to willful inattention, true ignorance, or subconscious denial, it seems he did not. Regarding the death of Judah's sons, one commentator remarks, "[Judah] is living in a place of deep darkness and rebellion, and God has to use the radical means of killing his sons to keep him within reach. . . . Judah is oblivious to how much his life and choices are being opposed by God."[20] That's a harsh assessment, wouldn't you agree?

> Compare Genesis 38:10 with Genesis 38:7, 6:5, and 6:8, which are all printed on the next page. What common principle is depicted in all four verses? For each verse, circle the keyword(s) that reflect this common principle.

Day Four / Week Three

The LORD saw that the wickedness of man was great in the earth, and that every intention of the thoughts of his heart was only evil continually. (Gen. 6:5)

But Noah found favor in the eyes of the LORD. (Gen. 6:8)

But Er, Judah's firstborn, was wicked in the sight of the LORD, and the LORD put him to death. (Gen. 38:7)

And what he did was wicked in the sight of the LORD, and he put him to death also. (Gen. 38:10)

Whether Judah was blind to his sons' wickedness or simply chose to turn a blind eye, God sees everything. The concept of the Lord "seeing" is the common thread shared in the four verses. This idea of "seeing" continues even further into Genesis 38, which we will explore beginning in Week Four.

Read Genesis 38:11, and answer the questions. What promise is implied by Judah's words to Tamar?

Compare what Judah says to Tamar with what he is thinking, as revealed in the text. What does this suggest about Judah's true intentions?

How does Tamar respond to Judah's instructions? Circle one.

> She demands her levirate rights immediately.
>
> She runs away.
>
> She chases after another man.
>
> She pleads with Judah not to send her away.
>
> She obeys and goes back to her father's house.

Lessons from God's Flood

> "And we know that for those who love God all things work together for good, for those who are called according to his purpose." —Romans 8:28

What might Tamar's response to Judah's command suggest about her character?

Imagine being in Tamar's sandals. Describe two or three struggles she may have been experiencing.

Though Tamar is sent back to her father's house, she would still have been under Judah's authority. In that time, when a bride price was paid, the bride was in effect purchased by the family. Judah could have kept Tamar in his home until his youngest son was ready to marry, but instead, Judah sends her away. The writer points out that Judah "feared [his son] would die" (Gen. 38:11). The writer expects us to realize that Judah had no intention of giving his last living son to Tamar. The less-than-praiseworthy character we have witnessed thus far from Judah has not changed. His rebellion against God (in marrying a Canaanite) and his repeated deceptions are presented in stark contrast to young Tamar's submission and obedience. Judah gives Tamar to Onan, and she stays. He tells her to return home, and she goes. What neither Tamar nor Judah realize is that, through it all, God is watching and working.

YOUR TURN

For his eyes are on the ways of a man, and he sees all his steps.

Job 34:21

Read Job 34:21 above. What difference do you think it would make in the world if God did not see all?

Think back on the past few weeks; what one way has this truth (that God sees all) made a difference in your life personally? Write a prayer of gratitude in the margin.

Day Four / Week Three

Where in your life right now do you need assurance that God sees your need? Bring your requests to God in prayer.

Is there a particular area of your life right now you wish God didn't see? Is there something you need to confess? Bring your struggles to God, and ask for His help. He already knows everything you are facing and is eager to lead you to a place of restoration.

DAY FIVE
Trapped in a Waiting Game

Yesterday, we left off with young Tamar being sent back to her father's house, supposedly until Judah sends for her once his youngest son grows up.

Reread Genesis 38:11, and answer the questions that follow.

Who did Judah speak with? Circle all that apply.

    Tamar's father   Shelah   Tamar

Consider those Judah does not speak with. How might this further expose Judah's true intentions?

How does Judah describe Tamar's status as he sends her away? Circle one.

    widowed   betrothed

Lessons from God's Flood

If Judah has no intention of giving his third son to Tamar but commands Tamar to wait for him to grow up, where would this leave Tamar? How does her future look? What options does she have?

Poor Tamar. Married to not one but two evil men, then twice widowed, all likely before her sixteenth birthday. As if that were not enough, she is sent home and told to wait for Judah's third son to grow up. But you and I know that Judah has no intention of giving his third son to Tamar. In effect, Judah has banished her to permanent childlessness and widowhood—a near worthless status in that day for a woman.

PAUSE TO PONDER

> Compare Tamar's day and culture with the culture you live in today. What gains have women enjoyed? What costs (and/or losses) have accompanied the changes? In what way(s) can you sympathize with Tamar?

Up to this point in the story, what have we witnessed of Tamar? For each pair, circle which one is true based on what we have read of the story so far.

Tamar speaks up	Tamar is silent
Tamar is passive	Tamar is active
Tamar is obedient	Tamar is disobedient

Though we have just scratched the surface of the story, we have already learned much about Tamar. She has endured so much, yet she never retaliates, never manipulates, never runs away. One commentator writes that "after the death of both sons, [the fact that Tamar] hoped for the growing-up of the third, Shelah, seems to point her out as a woman of extraordinary character."[21] Some might agree; others may not.

Day Five / Week Three

How about you? Do you agree with the quote in the previous paragraph? Share your thoughts.

The Stage Is Set

Genesis 38 comprises thirty verses. So far in our study, we have completed our journey through roughly one-third of the chapter. Much has taken place in those first eleven verses. Nevertheless, their primary purpose in the narrative is to serve as the background for the rest of the chapter. The events are critical and certainly heartbreaking, but they are not the primary focus of the chapter, as we will soon discover. This is important to keep in mind because if we attempt to place too much emphasis where the writer does not intend it, we risk misunderstanding what God is trying to teach us through His Word.

Even so, I know that many readers, perhaps even you, have suffered the nightmare of abuse, including sexual abuse, at one time or another. I would never want to gloss over those heartaches.

When I think back on my own story and consider what God has taught me over the years, I marvel at how often He used the most painful events to teach me some of the deepest truths about Himself. From time to time, I will revisit these life lessons by reading through my old journals. For the past twenty years, I have kept journals, recording my thoughts and prayers and conversations with God. In one of those journals, I wrote these words:

> *July 10, 2015. Lord, if I found the courage to give myself fully to a broken, abusive man . . . how could I not give myself fully to You? . . . What can man do that You cannot redeem for Your glory? Behold, the Cross! . . .*

> Bible study tip: if we place too much emphasis where the biblical writer does not intend it, we risk misunderstanding what God is trying to teach us through His Word.

> "In God I trust; I shall not be afraid. What can man do to me?" —Psalm 56:11

PAUSE TO PONDER

Read Psalm 56:11 in the margin. How have you seen this principle at work in your own life? How has God proven Himself trustworthy to you? Take a few moments to give Him praise for His faithfulness.

Lessons from God's Flood

Earlier, I mentioned that the first third of Genesis 38 serves as background for the rest.

In your Bible, highlight or mark each occurrence of the word *time* in Genesis 38. (Hint: you should find three.)

Next, complete the table as follows. In the second column, write which verses encompass each time segment that you marked in your Bible. In the third column, write the total number of verses included in each time segment. In the last column, write the approximate span of time in which the events would have taken place. I completed the first time segment for you. (Hint: keep in mind that the events in Genesis 38 span a total of twenty-one years, as based on our calculations from the end of Week Two.)

Time Segments	Which verses are included?	Total Number of Verses	Total Time (Approximate)
First	1–11	11	19 years
Second			
Third			

How do the time segments provide insight into what the writer may be emphasizing in the text?

In Scripture, the repetition of words or concepts can often provide further insight into the structure of a passage, meaning of a text, or something the writer may be trying to emphasize. Genesis 38 is divided into three time segments, each of which is significantly more detailed than the last while covering an ever decreasing segment of time. This severe slowing down of time in order to recount the details as the story progresses gives us a strong indication as to where the writer places the most importance. The first segment covers a span of approximately nineteen years. The second segment (verses 12–26) covers one to two years. The final segment (verses 27–30) likely occurred over a period of several hours or perhaps a day.

This means that the author devotes a full two-thirds of the chapter to events spanning barely 10 percent of the total time period. Not only that, but verse 12, where the second time marker appears, serves as a key turning point in the story.

Day Five / Week Three

Reread Genesis 38:1 and 38:12, which are both printed below. Using different types of marks, such as circles, boxes, or brackets (or different-color highlighters), identify parallel words, phrases, or concepts that appear in both verses.

It happened at that time that Judah went down from his brothers and turned aside to a certain Adullamite, whose name was Hirah. (Gen. 38:1)

In the course of time the wife of Judah, Shua's daughter, died. When Judah was comforted, he went up to Timnah to his sheepshearers, he and his friend Hirah the Adullamite. (Gen. 38:12)

In addition to the parallels you marked above, identify one set of opposite phrases.

Now that the background is set in Genesis 38:1–11, the author focuses on the next series of events. The first thing we are told is that some time has passed. This mention of "time" is the first parallel we see between verses 1 and 12. Next, you probably noticed that Judah's friend, Hirah the Adullamite, suddenly reappears. Finally, another link between verses 1 and 12 relates to direction. In verse 1, Judah left his father and family in mourning and "went down from his brothers . . . ," and in verse 12, after being comforted, he "went up to Timnah" to see his sheepshearers. But overseeing the shearing of his sheep was not the only reason he would have been there. In those days, after the sheepshearing work was finished, it would typically be followed by a time of celebration and revelry. In short, it was party time. It seems that, at this point, Judah has recovered from his grief.

Reread Genesis 38:12. What happens to Judah, and what happens next?

Judah has endured the loss of two sons and now a wife, but, after a required period of mourning, it seems he is ready to move on. That's not a bad thing; however, nothing in Scripture is random. The writer's choice of words, "When Judah was comforted," is meant to draw our minds back to what led Judah to depart from his family in the first place.

Lessons from God's Flood

Glance back at Genesis 37:34–35. Describe Judah's role in the events leading up to his father being so grief-stricken that he refused to be comforted. (Hint: see Gen. 37:26–32.)

Compare and contrast how Jacob responds to his loss in Genesis 37:34–35 with how Judah responds to his loss in Genesis 38:12. List both similarities and differences.

similarities	differences

 Is there anything you consider to be particularly striking? Explain.

While Judah is moving right along, we are reminded that his father is still suffering the loss of his son Joseph, the son whom Judah conspired to be sold into slavery. Not only is Jacob left hanging (so to speak) in a perpetual state of mourning, but Tamar, likewise due to Judah's deceit, is also left hanging in a perpetual state of mourning (widowhood). Meanwhile, Judah is headed to a party.

##############................YOUR TURN...............##############

Where in your life right now are you waiting on something? Maybe you're even waiting on God.

What is one lesson you have learned from Tamar's response to the events she has experienced that you could apply to your life?

Record one action step you will take this upcoming week.

If you have not completed the Day Three Pause to Ponder on page 112, do that now.

Lesson Summary

What scripture, statement, or thought was most significant to you this week?*
Write it down, and then reword it into a prayer of response to God.

*Share your favorite takeaway with a friend or on social media using #TamarBibleStudy. A worship song that captures what I imagine I might feel like if I were in Tamar's place at this point in her life is called "You Say," by Lauren Daigle.

Notes

[1] Or possibly near Adullam (same throughout the study whenever mention is made that Judah lived in Adullam).

[2] Based on Genesis 38:14, Tamar's father's home was likely within walking distance of Enaim to enable Tamar to accomplish her task and return home without raising suspicions. Enaim was a village situated between Adullam and Timnah. Chad Brand et al., eds., *Holman Illustrated Bible Dictionary* (Nashville: Holman Bible Publishers, 2003), s.v. "Enaim or Enam."

[3] Steven P. Carpenter, *The Story of Joseph and Judah: A Teacher's Narrative and Structural Commentary on Genesis 37–50* (Fort Lauderdale, FL: St. Andrews House, 2010), 20.

[4] David D. Pettus, "Tamar, Daughter-in-Law of Judah," in *Lexham Bible Dictionary*, ed. John D. Barry et al. (Bellingham, WA: Lexham Press, 2016).

[5] The letter *nun* in Hebrew has two forms: ן and נ.

Lessons from God's Flood

[6] Carpenter, *The Story of Joseph and Judah*, 20.

[7] Examples of seeking favor with people include Genesis 30:27; 32:5; 33:8, 10, 15; 34:11; 39:4; 47:25, 29; 50:4; examples of people seeking favor with God include Genesis 6:8; 18:3; 19:19; 39:21.

[8] In Genesis 34:4, the word translated *get*, as in, "Get me this girl for my wife," is also taken from the identical Hebrew verb.

[9] Carpenter, *The Story of Joseph and Judah*, 18.

[10] In that day, men ready to marry would often have some influence with their father as to who they wanted to marry, whereas women rarely had a voice. (Curiously, we find an exception with the marriage of Isaac and Rebekah. It was Rebekah, not Isaac, who was given the choice. See Gen. 24.)

[11] Carpenter, *The Story of Joseph and Judah*, 20.

[12] Richard R. Losch, *All the People in the Bible: An A–Z Guide to the Saints, Scoundrels, and Other Characters in Scripture* (Grand Rapids: William B. Eerdmans, 2008), 415.

[13] Jocelyn McWhirter, "Marriage," in *Lexham Bible Dictionary*.

[14] Rob Fleenor, "Law, Levirate," in *Lexham Bible Dictionary*.

[15] This would occur in cases in which the widow's family refused to take her in.

[16] This could occur in cases in which the family of the deceased husband refuses to pay the debt on the widow's behalf.

[17] Nahum M. Sarna, *The JPS Torah Commentary: Genesis* (Philadelphia: Jewish Publication Society, 1989), 267.

[18] William MacDonald, *Believer's Bible Commentary: Old and New Testaments*, ed. Arthur Farstad (Nashville: Thomas Nelson, 1995), 72.

[19] Some have proposed that God's divine judgement on Onan is due to the practice of birth control in general; however, it is important to recognize that the emphasis of the narrative is on Onan's levirate duty.

[20] Carpenter, *The Story of Joseph and Judah*, 20.

[21] John Peter Lange et al., *A Commentary on the Holy Scriptures: Genesis* (Bellingham, WA: Logos Bible Software, 2008), 592.

NOTES

NOTES

PART II

ABIDING

NOTES

TRUSTING IN FAVOR

WEEK FOUR

WHEN WE LAST READ OF TAMAR, WE DISCOVERED THAT Judah had no intention of giving her his third son in marriage. Though she is innocent of any wrongdoing, Tamar seems abandoned to a life as a childless widow—a tragedy in that society—but does this mean God has abandoned her as well?

Tamar will soon learn of Judah's betrayal. When she does, she decides to take matters into her own hands. Some call her courageous; others urge condemnation. Either way, her choices forever alter the trajectory of her life and pave the way for the coming Messiah.

DAY ONE
Facing Your "Impossible"

After I graduated from seminary, God blessed me with the perfect part-time job. Not only were the schedule and income exactly what I needed, but I could not have asked for a more enjoyable boss. She was intelligent and kind, and she cared not just about work-related matters but was genuinely considerate of my personal needs as well. Although it was a secular organization, my boss (and most of my coworkers) knew why I took the job. It allowed me to simultaneously pay my bills

(as long as I kept my expenses low) and chase the dream God had placed in my heart to write and teach.

One day, my boss invited me to join her for a walk outdoors. The office building was situated near a quiet residential area of lush trees and manicured lawns. Afternoon walks were my favorite part of the day. Though the invitation to walk with my boss was rare, I thought nothing of it—until she broke the news. She had put in her resignation. I stopped midstride as my mouth fell open. "No!" my mind protested. "You can't leave!" I had been working for her less than a year and now she was leaving? Seeing the dejected look on my face, she explained she was changing careers to do something she had always wanted to do. Though I was happy for her, I was thoroughly disappointed to see her go. To add insult to injury, I learned that her decision was partly my fault. When I asked her why she was leaving, she smiled and answered, "You inspired me."

She went on to explain how my sacrifices and efforts to prioritize my life and time and decisions around the pursuit of my dream inspired her to chase after her own. Later that evening, I was talking with my mom on the phone. I shared the day's events, along with my deep disappointment that the boss whom I had come to appreciate so much was leaving. My mom listened quietly, after which she simply responded, "Next time, inspire someone at work you don't like." I couldn't help but laugh. Looking back, I'm not sure if she was trying to be funny, but to this day, her words still make me chuckle.

Throughout our lives, people will come and go. The events might be positive (like my boss pursuing her dreams—in truth, I was happy for her) or painful (such as when we lose someone we love). Although we may not always understand why God allows things to happen, behind it all is a sovereign God lovingly watching over His children, His creation, and, ultimately, His plan of redemption.

God Fashions Our Days for a Purpose

On the first day of our study, we read Matthew 1:1–3, where Tamar's name is listed in the lineage of Christ. That's a significant fact, especially considering how rare it is for women to be named in most biblical genealogies.

Read Psalm 139:16 in the margin. Rewrite these truths in your own words.

"Your eyes saw my unformed [body]; in your book were written, every one of them, the days that were formed for me, when as yet there was none of them."
—Psalm 139:16

The word translated *formed* in Psalm 139:16 stems from the Hebrew root word *yatsar*, which relates to creating or fashioning something for a purpose. The first time this word appears in Scripture is in Genesis 2:7.

Write Genesis 2:7 below.

The same word appears in Isaiah 64:8. Fill in the blank with the missing word, which also stems from the Hebrew root word *yatsar*.

"But now, O Lord, you are our Father; we are the clay, and you are our _____; we are all the work of your hand."

Consider Psalm 139:16 along with Genesis 2:7 and Isaiah 64:8. What difference would it make if God were not actively involved in shaping your life for a purpose?

PAUSE TO PONDER

> Take a few moments to meditate on the fact that your heavenly Father fashions each one of your days with a purpose. How might your life be different if you began each day embracing this truth with eager expectation?

God also fashioned Tamar's days for a purpose, which means it was His will to include Tamar in the lineage of Christ. This does not mean God wills the sin and suffering that Tamar encountered on the way, but because He is sovereign, everything in the end will conform to His perfect will. When we take a few moments to pause and reflect on this truth, we get our first glimpse into the overarching beauty of God's plan as He weaves Tamar into His grand redemption story.

Trusting in God's Favor

The Last Thread of Hope

Before we move forward, let's do a quick review of what we have learned of Tamar's life up to this point. For each sentence below, fill in the blanks with one of the keywords (note: some keywords are used more than once).

widow   Judah   dead   withholding   teenager   wicked

Tamar is barely a young _____ when she is married.

Her first husband is _____ and God strikes him _____.

Tamar marries Judah's second son, but he also is _____ and struck _____.

_____ commands Tamar to "remain a _____ in your father's house, till Shelah my son grows up."

Scripture alludes to Judah's true intention of _____ his son Shelah from Tamar.

Consider all that has happened so far; where does this leave Tamar?

> "You have . . . put my tears in your bottle. Are they not in your book?"
> —Psalm 56:8

At this point, Tamar is living in her father's house, holding on to Judah's promise that young Shelah would be given to her in marriage. Can you imagine her conflicting thoughts? As much as she would have wanted to have a place in Judah's household and enjoy the blessing of raising children, surely she wrestled with the fear that Shelah would be no better than his brothers. If worrying about her future were not difficult enough, picture what that season of waiting may have been like for Tamar. She likely had friends, brothers, and sisters who were married and starting families. Some might be living alongside her in her father's house or nearby.

As time continues slipping by, Tamar is still holding onto hope that her day of raising a family of her own will come. Did she hide her pain while surrounded by her young nieces and nephews? Did she have anyone to confide in? Did anyone among her family or friends suspect Tamar was to blame for her circumstances—or worse, consider her cursed? After all, not only did both of her husbands die, but she was left with no child. We don't know the answers to these questions, but this we do know: God saw Tamar's suffering.

Day One / Week Four

God sees everything. He saw the wickedness of Er and Onan. He knows the secret thoughts of Judah—that he has no intention of giving his youngest son to Tamar. While God is working through human history to accomplish His eternal purposes, He also takes notice of every detail of our lives. Though Tamar may not have known the one true God at this point, God knew her. He created her for a purpose, and nothing could get in His way.

> After Judah banishes young Tamar to lifelong widowhood, a period of time passes. What is the next event Scripture records, according to the first part of Genesis 38:12?

As we discussed at the end of last week's lesson, Genesis 38:12 parallels Genesis 38:1, but with one key difference. In verse 1, we read that Judah left his father in perpetual mourning and "went down" from his family, but in verse 12, he quickly recovered from his own loss and "went up" to enjoy a party. The introduction of a new time segment, along with the shift in direction, serves as a turning point in the story. Curiously, the event that sets this turning point in motion is the death of Judah's wife.

In last week's lesson, we spent some time briefly examining the practice of levirate marriage; however, we did not cover everything. According to the *Lexham Bible Dictionary* (and affirmed by numerous other resources), the fulfillment of levirate marriage was not limited to the deceased husband's brother. Instead, "It was the duty of the nearest male relative of a deceased man to marry the childless widow and to father her children."[1] Keep this in mind as we move forward in the story.

> Considering all that has transpired in Tamar's life thus far, what might be the significance of the passing of Judah's wife at this point in the story? (Hint: consider the definition of levirate marriage.)

God does not delight in the death of anyone (Ezek. 18:32), but the tragic fallout of sin means that on this side of heaven, death eventually comes to everyone. Is it merely coincidence that Judah's wife dies while Judah has deceptively abandoned Tamar to a life without a husband, a family, or a future? Or is there more going on *behind the seen*?

> Read Genesis 38:13-14. What does Tamar realize concerning Judah's youngest son, Shelah?

"I form light and create darkness; I make well-being and create calamity; I am the Lord, who does all these things."
—Isaiah 45:7

With Tamar's first and second husbands dead and Judah's only remaining son withheld from her, Tamar is faced with a tremendous crisis in light of the culture in which she lives.

Imagine being Tamar; how might you have responded? Circle all that resonate or write your own.

despair   bitterness   anger   revenge   resignation
acceptance   take action   other: _____

Consider your response to the last question. Is your answer based on past experience or lessons learned? Explain.

At this point, Shelah was clearly of marriageable age, but Judah had not come back for Tamar. Perhaps Judah hoped to prevent Shelah from marrying at all (it may not have been too difficult to convince the boy, considering how it turned out for his brothers). Or maybe a secret betrothal had been arranged.[2] Either way, it may seem as if all hope is gone for Tamar, but I love what Jesus says to His disciples in Matthew 19:26: "with God all things are possible."

> "Behold, I am the LORD, the God of all flesh. Is anything too hard for me?"
> —Jeremiah 32:27

................YOUR TURN................

For each verse in the table, record the "impossible" situation and God's response (as spoken by the Lord or God's messenger).

	Describe the "impossible" situation.	What encouragement is spoken and by whom?
Genesis 18:11-14		
Matthew 19:24-26		
Luke 1:26-37		

Day One / Week Four

How have you witnessed God transform the "impossible" into "possible" in your life?

If you cannot recall a time when God stepped in and turned around an "impossible" situation, take a few moments to ask God to reveal how He has been at work in your life. Write a prayer of thanksgiving.

What would you say to someone who does not believe that God performs miracles today? Who can you encourage today with a reminder of these truths?

DAY TWO
Sizing Up Your Options

Yesterday, we read that Tamar had discovered Judah's deception. His youngest son had grown up but had not been given to her as she was led to believe. During all that time, because Tamar was basically "owned" by Judah, she had little choice but to wait and trust that Judah would do the right thing and come for her. Up to this point, Tamar's life and circumstances had essentially been controlled by her father and father-in-law, but things were about to change.

Friends Watching Your Back

Reread Genesis 38:13-14. How does the person refer to Judah?

Why might the use of this designation of Judah be important? What does this convey about how the community (or at a minimum, the person who spoke to Tamar) views Tamar's status in relation to Judah?

List two or three reasons someone may have had for wanting to inform Tamar of Judah's activity.

The expression in Genesis 38:13 translated "Tamar was told" (or "it was told to Tamar") is interesting in Hebrew. The verb is *yug-gad*, and it comes from the Hebrew root word *nagad*, meaning *conspicuous*. One commentator explains that the word, as it's used in Genesis 38:13,

> is in the passive form, which is not common in Biblical Hebrew. The atmosphere here is that the person who spoke with Tamar did this in order to prompt her into action. [In other words, informing Tamar of Judah's activities] was not told simply for the sake of general knowledge. After all, there is nothing special about Judah's action. . . . [Rather,] the Bible hints . . . of something underhanded being done.[3]

"For [God] knows the secrets of the heart."

—Psalm 44:21

Even before we read of Tamar taking any action, Scripture alludes to the fact that something is not right, and the responsible party is Judah.

PAUSE TO PONDER

Read Hebrews 4:12–13 and Psalm 44:21 in the margin. Do you find comfort in knowing that God sees the secret intentions, thoughts, or feelings others may have (or have had) against you? Why or why not? How do these verses challenge you in light of the secret intentions, thoughts, or feelings you may have (or have had) against others? Why is confessing not only our sinful actions but also our sinful thoughts important? (Optional: see Romans 12:2 and 2 Corinthians 10:5.)

Day Two / Week Four

Even if Judah thinks his actions will not be found out, God sees everything. Let's examine Genesis 38:14 more closely by dividing it into three parts, which we will tackle in reverse order.

> In the last part of Genesis 38:14, what wording does the author use to describe Tamar's discovery? Using a Bible that adheres to a more literal translation (such as the English Standard Version, New American Standard Bible, King James Version, or New King James Version), fill in the blanks.
>
> For she _____ that Shelah was grown up, and she had not been _____ to him in marriage.
>
> Where did Tamar go according to the middle of Genesis 38:14? Be specific.

Even the name of the town is significant to the story. In the first column below, trace the word *Enaim* in Hebrew. In the second column, trace the Hebrew word that means *sight*. In the third column, write the Hebrew lettering that the words share in common.

Trace the word *Enaim* in Hebrew.	Trace the Hebrew word that means *sight*.	Write the Hebrew lettering that the words share in common.
עֵינַיִם	עַיִן	

- What conclusions can you draw based on what you observed in the tracing exercise?

The root word used in the Hebrew place name *Enaim* is *ayin*, meaning *eye*. It is the exact same root word used in Genesis 38:7 and 38:10 for "sight" in "the sight of the LORD." The word *Enaim* means *two eyes*.[4] Nothing in Scripture is random. The idea of "seeing" runs throughout the narrative, starting from the beginning, when Judah "saw" the daughter of a certain Canaanite.

But Enaim is not the only place name that provides us with some insight into what is happening in the narrative. Setting aside the generic references to

Canaanites and Adullamites, there are a total of three specific place names included in Genesis 38; each one is informative.

> Glance back at Genesis 38:5. Write the meaning of the name *Chezib*. (Hint: if you don't remember, refer back to page 88.)

> How does the meaning of this city's name relate to the events that we have studied so far?

After Chezib, the next location named in the story is Enaim, meaning *two eyes*. Recall God's judgment on all humans for the wickedness in Genesis 6, where we read that, "The LORD saw that the wickedness of man was great in the earth" (Gen. 6:5). Consider also God seeing and judging the wickedness of Judah's sons: "Er, Judah's firstborn, was wicked in the sight of the LORD . . . . And what [Onan] did was wicked in the sight of the LORD, and he put him to death also" (Gen. 38:7, 10).

> Do you think it is significant that Tamar positioned herself at the entrance of a place named "two eyes"? Explain.

> "'The LORD is my portion,' says my soul, 'therefore I will hope in him.'"
> —Lamentations 3:24

The last specific location named in the narrative is Timnah. The meaning of *Timnah* is *allotted portion*.[5] The name stems from the Hebrew root word *manah*, meaning to count, number, or appoint. When we consider all that Tamar has endured so far—being married to men who were both "wicked in the sight of the LORD," twice widowed, childless, sent away, followed by Judah's deception in holding back his third son—the concept of allotted portion offers a glimmer of hope, but the road ahead will be anything but easy.

Things Are Not as They Appear

Because I did not grow up going to church, as a child, Halloween seemed a harmless opportunity to dress up like someone or something else in order to amass delicious treats. I will never forget the Halloween when I was six years old. My mother had worked for weeks sewing the costume I asked for. Finally, the long-awaited day arrived. My mother dressed me in my full-length black witch costume, painted my face green, and topped it all off with a big, black pointy hat. I was so excited! I could hardly wait to see how I looked. After she finished the final touches and was satisfied everything was perfect, she let me loose. I ran straight to the bathroom, where I took one look in the mirror and burst into tears. Bewildered, my mother rushed to my side. "Sweetheart, what's wrong?"

Sobbing uncontrollably, I stammered, "Mommy, I'm ugly!"

Mom didn't remind me I had asked to be a witch. She didn't try to talk me into liking the costume she had worked so hard to create. She didn't even scold me for the likelihood this would make us all late. I only remember her tenderly bending down to ask me one question: "Honey, what do you want to be?"

"A princess," I sniveled, as her fingers wiped away my tears.

Performing a mental inventory of all her sewing and craft supplies, she looked back down into my tear-stained face. "How about I make you into a beautiful bride?" To this day, I still don't know how she transformed her black-caped, green-streaked, sad little witch into a white-laced, blushing, flower-laden bride, but she did. In the end, I had the perfect costume, and there was still plenty of time to gather a pile of yummy treats.

Deceiving the Deceiver

> *[Tamar] took off her widow's garments and covered herself with a veil, wrapping herself up . . .*
>
> Genesis 38:14

Based on the chronology we outlined at the end of last week's lesson, roughly a year had gone by during which Judah was widowed and recovered from his grief. At this point, Tamar was likely about fifteen or sixteen years old.

Complete the table by contrasting Tamar's experience of being widowed with Judah's. In the last rows, record any additional contrasts you can think of. I completed one for you.

	Tamar	Judah
Was s/he free to remarry (yes or no)?	No	
Was the period of being a widow/widower long or short (in contrast to the other person's)?		
Did the period of mourning come to an end (yes or no)?		
Other:_____		
Other:_____		

"Do not be deceived: God is not mocked, for whatever one sows, that will he also reap." —Galatians 6:7

Trusting in God's Favor

How would you summarize the contrast between Tamar and Judah's respective experiences with being widowed?

Which aspect of Tamar's widowhood disheartens you the most? Why?

Tamar and Judah's experiences could not be more different. In addition to the contrasts in the table, there was also a vast difference in age when Tamar and Judah each became widowed. Furthermore, given the young age of Tamar's husbands, their deaths would have been unexpected in contrast to the passing of Judah's wife. Perhaps the most tragic aspect is the fact that Judah is free to move on, while Tamar is still trapped. When she learned of Judah's betrayal, she could have withered in despair or languished in bitterness. Instead, we discover Tamar to be resilient. Refusing to sit by and do nothing, she decides to take matters into her own hands.

Using a Bible that adheres to a more literal translation (such as the English Standard Version, New American Standard Bible, New King James Version, or King James Version), read Genesis 38:14-19 (verse 14 is a review). What did Tamar do, according to Genesis 38:14? Be specific.

Apart from Genesis 38:14 and 38:19, the Hebrew word *tsaiph*, translated *veil*, appears in only one other verse in the entire Old Testament. Read Genesis 24:51 and 61-67. Who covered herself with a veil, and what were the events that prompted her to take this action?

Thinking again about Tamar's story, list two or three reasons Tamar may have decided to veil herself. Stated another way, what are some possible outcomes Tamar might have been aiming for in her encounter with Judah?

Commentators are divided in their opinions as to whether Tamar's actions were noble, reprehensible, or somewhere in between. How about you? In light of Tamar's situation and the restrictions she faced in that time and culture, what is your opinion of Tamar's actions at this point in our study?

In Week One, we learned that it was customary for an unmarried woman to veil herself in the presence of her future husband. This is why Rebekah veiled herself upon approaching Isaac in Genesis 24, as he was soon to become her husband. Leah also would have been veiled when she was passed off as her sister Rachel when given in marriage to Jacob. Concerning Tamar, the *ESV Study Bible* notes that Tamar "covers herself with a veil, possibly intending at first to remind Judah that she is betrothed to Shelah."[6] While the idea briefly crossed my mind as one possibility when I initially studied the passage, we simply do not know. What we do know is that the first thought that crossed Judah's mind was something altogether different.

YOUR TURN

We are now a bit more than halfway through our study. You have certainly been working hard these past weeks. It is my prayer that God would use His marvelous, living Word to speak to your heart and mind as you explore the story of Tamar. Surely the Lord is pleased with your efforts! The psalmist writes, "Oh how I love your law! It is my meditation all the day" (Ps. 119:97).

So far in your journey through Tamar's story, what have you found to be most surprising? Encouraging? Strange or Confusing?

Trusting in God's Favor

In what way(s) has God been speaking to you personally through His Word and Tamar's story? Is there something He keeps bringing to your mind or pressing on your heart?

Write a prayer of gratitude for how God has been working in your life and speaking through His Word since you began this study.

> Interesting Fact: In biblical times, widows' clothing was not distinguished by color but by material, such as sackcloth—a sign of mourning.

DAY THREE
Stepping into the Unknown

"She took off her widow's garments, covered herself with a veil, wrapping herself up, and sat at the entrance to Enaim" (Gen. 38:14). You and I can only imagine the level of desperation that Tamar had reached to take such steps. One scholar suggests that the reason Scripture specifically mentions that Tamar covered her face (verse 15) could be that she was ashamed of finding herself in a situation in which she sees no other recourse than to become like a prostitute.[7] Whatever drove her to such actions, her decision was made.

The encounter on the roadside likely took place upon Judah's return from (rather than his journey to) Timnah.[8] This would have not only provided Tamar time to consider her options, but it would also explain the absence of his friend Hirah. Either way, Tamar waited for her father-in-law, who would be returning from (or looking forward to) several days of celebration and festivities in Timnah. And it is here where we realize that Tamar's garments are not the only thing about her that has changed.

Before we move ahead in our story, let's glance back at some "family photos" of key events that have occurred within recent generations of this highly favored yet dysfunctional family. Using the references, complete the table. I filled in the first row for you.

Reference	Who was deceived?	Who was the deceiver? (Include any accomplices.)
Genesis 27:1–11, 15–27	Isaac	Jacob (and Rebekah)
Genesis 29:16–26		
Genesis 37:12–13, 23–33		
Genesis 38:13–15		

Consider the manner in which each person was deceived. What common thread do you notice?

Next, fill in the blanks with the keyword that best completes each sentence.

    favor   husband   seed   blessing

Jacob sought the _____ due the firstborn son.

Leah (and her father) sought to secure her a _____, being that she was the firstborn daughter.

Leah's sons were jealous for the _____ Jacob showered on Rachel's firstborn son.

Tamar sought Judah's _____ in order to secure her place in the family and continue the line of the firstborn son.

Reflect on the events outlined in the previous questions. Do you consider any of the deceivers justified in their motivations and/or actions? Explain.

A Common Thread

What a strange series of events! From one generation to the next, we find deceit and betrayal. Every scenario shares at least one common thread, figuratively and literally. They all involve clothing as a disguise or deception (the theme of clothing runs throughout the entire narrative). First, it was Jacob dressed like his

Trusting in God's Favor

brother Esau. Then Leah, hidden beneath her veil, is passed off as her younger sister Rachel. Next is Judah and his brothers dipping Joseph's garment in blood to deceive their father. In each case, the deceivers' aim relates to the blessings and privileges afforded to the firstborn (even a firstborn daughter had a few rights, as it turns out).

And then there is Tamar. She follows the pattern of disguising herself with garments, and her actions would carry on the line of Judah's firstborn, but what about the driving force underneath it all? Does she fit the pattern of being motivated by lust, greed, or envy, or were her motives justifiable? Let's see what we can find out.

Read Genesis 38:15-17 to get an overview of the passage.

In verse 16, we read that Judah "turned to her at the roadside." Here again, we come across the Hebrew verb *yet*. It is the same verb we examined in Week Two in our review of Genesis 38:1. If you recall, this verb refers to a change in direction but often includes an aspect of turning in the metaphorical sense, including deviating from a path of loyalty or righteousness. Here we see Judah heading one way and then, spying a lone woman sitting at the roadside (which usually signaled prostitution), he turns and heads toward her.

Consider the initial exchange between Judah and Tamar; who solicited who?

 - Do you think this is significant? Why or why not?

How does Judah approach the situation? Circle all that apply.

    He offers a friendly greeting.

    He avoids her and hurries on his way.

    He pauses to contemplate his options.

    He inquires about her intentions.

    He asks her name.

    He solicits her for sex.

In Day Three of Week Two, in response to Judah's decision to marry a Canaanite, I asked the following question: What appears to be the motivating force behind Judah's decisions up to this point of his life (flesh or spirit)?

Since then, roughly twenty years of Judah's life have passed.

Which of the following words would you use to describe Judah's character, actions, or motivations at this point in his life? Circle as many as you like, or fill in your own.

    bold   greedy   brave   desperate   wicked   wise   opportunistic   foolish   other:_____

Has anything changed for Judah? Explain.

How about Tamar? Which words would you use to describe Tamar's character, actions, or motivations at this point in the story? Circle as many as you like, or fill in your own.

    bold   greedy   brave   desperate   wicked   wise   opportunistic   foolish   other:_____

Do you think Tamar has changed from when she first married? If so, how?

Regrets

As much as I cringe at Judah's decisions and Tamar's desperation, if I take an honest look at my own past, I cringe even more. In my last year of high school, I made some new friends. One evening, they invited me to go with them to a nightclub. I could never have imagined how that one decision would alter the trajectory of my life. In less than a year, I found myself submerged in another world—a world of nightclubs, drinking, drugs, and, I am ashamed to confess it, sex with near strangers. Even as I write these words, I am silently praying, pleading with God that He would change His mind and not ask me to share these things. But He is asking, so I keep writing.

I do not remember most of the names of the men I slept with during those depraved years so long ago, but God does. One day, a few years ago, God asked me to confess to Him each encounter, each piece of my heart the enemy had stolen. As I confessed my sin to God, I poured out my heart onto the pages of my journal:

> *All I wanted was for someone to want me. It seemed that sex was all there was. No one seemed to notice or care where I was or if I came home . . . oh God, look at the filth! Look at who I was! A horror and unloved!*

Immediately, God spoke to my spirit, "NO! Look at who you are now."

I continued writing, "I am sorry, Lord, for defiling the body you created for me—for forfeiting the desires you had for me. Yet, I praise you for what you can do with the ashes. I praise you for all that you will do with these ashes. I give these ashes to you, oh Lord, and you will turn them into royal robes fitting for a bride—a pure and spotless bride for the King." These words still stir my heart when I read them today. For each one of us, our sin—no matter what it is—is no match for the infinite, eternal mercy of God.

If we belong to Christ, our past no longer defines us. Our old self has died and has been buried, and we have been raised to new life in Christ. The things that you and I are deeply ashamed of were never God's desire for us, but if we are willing to surrender them into His holy, nail-scarred hands, He will redeem all of it for His glory. God wastes nothing.

> **PAUSE TO PONDER**
>
> God wastes nothing. Do you agree? Through the prophet Isaiah, God promises that His people will be given "a crown of beauty instead of ashes . . . a garment of praise instead of a spirit of despair . . . . Instead of your shame you will receive a double portion" (Isa. 61:3, 7 NIV). How has God turned ashes into beauty in your life? Are there any ashes, despair, or shame that you need to surrender to God today? Will you trust His promises, knowing that He has reserved for you "a crown of beauty," "a garment of praise," and even "a double portion"? Write a praise to God for what He has done and for what He will do.

> Our sin—no matter what it is—is no match for the infinite, eternal mercy of God.

> When we surrender our regrets into Christ's nail-scarred hands, He will redeem them for His great glory. God wastes nothing.

Seizing an Opportunity

Just as my immoral lifestyle would have been evident to others, it would seem that Tamar had learned some things about her father-in-law's less-than-praiseworthy character as well. Perhaps she decided to use it to her advantage. The *CSB Study Bible* notes say, "In order to get Judah to fulfill his family's obligation to produce an heir for Er and remove the stigma of her childlessness, Tamar apparently took advantage of her father-in-law's immoral character."[9]

Recognizing that she had few options, Tamar may have fully intended to deceive Judah into thinking she was a prostitute. Or, as we explored previously, some scholars propose that she may have veiled herself at first in the hope of reminding Judah of his promise to give her Shelah, but when Judah mistook her for a roadside prostitute, she recognized a window of opportunity and decided to play along. The one thing we do know is that Tamar aimed to do *something*.

> Consider Tamar's not-so-distant past. After her marriage (and widowhood) to Judah's wicked son, Er, how was she treated by Onan after Judah insisted he marry her? Circle one.
>
>   wife   prostitute
>
> What role might Tamar's experiences while living in Judah's home have played in her actions in Genesis 38:14-16?
>
> Do you think her actions are justified? Why or why not?

Until this point, Tamar had little choice other than to be obedient and patient. However, when she discovers Judah's deception and betrayal, she realizes she is the victim of yet another injustice. While she did have rights under the levirate practice, as a woman, she would have needed someone to stand in her defense, presumably her father. Sadly, no one steps forward.

But circumstances have changed. The fact that Judah is now a widower offers Tamar another opportunity. After all, the levirate practice was not limited to a brother of the deceased husband but the closest male relative. When Tamar is told where Judah would be traveling, she realizes this is her chance—perhaps her only chance. Tamar could have simply stayed home and surrendered to her fate. Given

Trusting in God's Favor

> "The LORD ... looked for justice, but behold, bloodshed; for righteousness, but behold, an outcry!"
>
> —Isaiah 5:7

the culture of the time, in which women were virtually powerless, for Tamar to have the mindset to step up and do something, even in the face of true injustice, would have been a rare quality among women in that day.

YOUR TURN

How about today? Do you think women in our culture are more willing to stand up for themselves in the face of personal injustice? Explain.

Where in your life have you experienced (or are you currently experiencing) a personal injustice?

Do you believe God was (is) actively working in the situation, even if you cannot see it? Explain.

What are you grateful for in your life right now?

How can you take comfort in knowing that God is sovereign in all circumstances? Write a prayer as God leads you.

DAY FOUR
Clinging to God's Promises

In the Bible, there are two Hebrew words that can be translated *prostitute*. One is *zona*, which refers to what we would think of as a street prostitute. The other word is *qadesh*, which refers to a cult (or shrine or temple) prostitute. Both words appear in Genesis 38 for a reason, as we will soon discover. Unlike cult prostitutes, *zonas* were paid little and treated with hardly more respect than stray dogs. Based on the original Hebrew text of Genesis 38:16, Judah saw Tamar and assumed her to be a *zona*.

Reread Genesis 38:16-17. What are Judah's first words to Tamar?

"Let me." Let *me*. For Judah, it's still all about "me." Here is a man who was willing to sell his brother, break his father's heart, abandon his family, even break the covenant with God almighty. Twenty years later, it seems that nothing has changed.

Contrast what Judah offers as payment in Genesis 38:17 with the words of Proverbs 6:26a, which reads, "for the price of a prostitute is only a loaf of bread." Why might Judah have offered so much? List as many reasons as you can think of.

More than Meets the Eye

On the surface, for Judah to offer a young goat to a *zona*, who would normally be paid a pittance, may seem nothing more than a reckless business transaction by a lonely man looking to satisfy his lust. However, we will soon discover that there is more going on here than meets the eye.

As for Tamar, prior to this point in the chapter, we see her being compliant and silent. Then, the first time we hear her speak, we realize she had learned something significant during her time of waiting: her father-in-law, the Hebrew, could not be trusted. We have also learned some things about Tamar. First, she is patient. She waited in her father's house. She waited for Shelah to grow up. She waited for Judah to keep his promise. However, when she realizes she is trapped in Judah's deception, we discover Tamar to be a young woman with the strength and courage to rise above her circumstances.

Trusting in God's Favor

PAUSE TO PONDER

> Describe a time when God gave you strength and courage to rise above your circumstances. What was the outcome? What impact did it have on your relationship with God? How about your relationship with others? Looking back, what are you most thankful for?

Compare Genesis 38:16 with 38:14. What wordplay seems to be at work? (Hint: look for a contrast in the last sentence of each verse.)

Solomon wrote in Ecclesiastes 3:7 that there is "a time to keep silence, and a time to speak." In the same way, we might add, there is a time to wait and a time to act. After waiting faithfully, Tamar realized she had not been given what Judah had promised (Gen. 38:14). The author's contrast in Genesis 38:14, "she had not been given" with 38:16, "what will you give me," is no accident. No more waiting. No more games. Now it is time to take action.

Judah responds, "I will send you a young goat from the flock." This was an outlandish price for a *zona*. After all, she was not offering an extravagant interlude at a high-end brothel; rather, this would have amounted to a few minutes in the dirt behind some bushes. Why would Judah pay so much? It seems unlikely that he was an overly generous man (after all, he sold his own brother for a few coins). Are these foolish words in a moment of weakness, or is there more to it? Being curious, I decided to do some research. Perhaps there were similar accounts in Scripture that might shed some light on the story. I decided to start with the goat.

At first, my efforts appeared to land at a dead end. Apart from Genesis 38:17, there is not a single reference in the Old Testament where a young goat is specifically offered as a payment for something. But then I discovered a handful of references where a young goat is given as a gift, and the particular events surrounding one of these occasions is telling. The story is found in the book of Judges.

Day Four / Week Four

In the space below, compare and contrast Genesis 38:12-17 with Judges 14:1-4 and Judges 15:1-2 (optional: read all of Judges 14:1–15:2). Record the similarities and differences you discover.

similarities	differences

What one thing between these two stories stands out to you the most? Why?

 Describe one or two ways the story of Samson and his wife helps shed light on the story of Judah and Tamar.

There are a number of striking parallels between these two accounts, perhaps the most obvious being that both stories take place near Timnah during a time of celebration (sheep shearing and wheat harvest). In Judges, we read that Samson brings a young goat to his wife as a gift. It seems that earlier, he had upset his wife and left in a rage (Judg. 14:5–19). Sometime later, however, he decides to return to his wife with a young goat. For you or me, roses or chocolate might be a better choice, but I digress. Either way, Samson expects that his gift would not only appease his wife but that it would also pave the way for sex. Upon his arrival, Samson discovers that his wife's father had given her to another man. Hoping to placate Samson, the father hastily offers Samson his younger daughter instead.

When we consider the events that make up the story of Samson (the location, the season, the young goat, the purpose of giving the goat, the betrayal and the offer of a younger sibling), the parallels to the story of Judah's encounter with Tamar could not be more striking.

Perhaps most noteworthy is that in the story of Samson, we read that God's hand is actively at work. Though God commanded His people to "be separate," God was willing to use Samson's weakness for women to fulfill His sovereign purposes.[10] Judges 14:4 says that Samson's insistence on marrying the Philistine woman "was

Trusting in God's Favor

from the LORD, for he was seeking an opportunity against the Philistines." Just as God had a purpose for Samson's marriage to the Philistine, God had a purpose for Judah's encounter with Tamar. In the one story, God's aim was to destroy Israel's enemies; in the other, it was to preserve the covenant family line. Who did God choose to fulfill that high calling? A mighty Israelite warrior? No. A teenage girl named Tamar.

To our modern sensibilities, for God to condone (and later, even bless!) the encounter between Judah and Tamar can be difficult to comprehend. After all, God would later institute laws that forbade a man from taking his daughter-in-law as a wife (Lev. 18:15). While we may find it difficult to approve of Tamar's actions, she had little choice after Judah's failure to give her to Shelah and restore her place in the family. Tamar's objective to conceive a child with Judah was in line with the intended purpose of the levirate customs at the time.

Read Genesis 38:17-18 (verse 17 is a review). What does Tamar demand for a pledge (or security), and how does Judah respond?

Read Hebrews 12:16-17. Compare and contrast Judah's actions in Genesis 38:18 with his uncle Esau's (see also Genesis 25:29-34). What might their actions suggest about their attitude toward God's unique covenant promises?

Compare Esau and Judah's actions with Tamar's. What value does Tamar seem to place on being a part of God's covenant family?

Stolen Identity

The items that Judah fairly throws at Tamar, a complete stranger and prostitute as far as he is concerned, would be equivalent to you or I handing over our social security card, along with copies of our signature and fingerprint, to a vagrant selling his wares on the street. (This reminds us of Judah's uncle Esau when he traded his birthright for a single meal.) The signet and staff Judah so willingly

Day Four / Week Four

surrendered were highly valuable, not because they were made of costly elements, such as silver or gold, but because of the power they held.

Like a fingerprint, the signet would leave a unique seal (imprint) on clay or wax, identifying its owner on legal documents and providing proof of ownership on his possessions. The staff was also significant. More than just a walking stick, it typically had a carved design at the top that uniquely identified its owner. The staff often symbolized authority (Exod. 4:1–5, 9:23; Isa. 10:24), and in time, the term evolved "to denote scepter and tribe.... In ancient Near Eastern iconography, the ruler's staff (often with a scepter) is a feature of royalty."[11]

In and of themselves, the signet and staff would not change anything for Tamar. However, having Judah's child would change everything. The signet, cord (likely used to carry the signet), and staff would provide Tamar the evidence she would need when the time came to reveal the identity of the child within. In effect, though Tamar had already been purchased by Judah as a wife for his son, thereby making her a permanent member of his family, she was abandoned and betrayed. By securing these items, Tamar would be prepared to reclaim identity with the family of Judah through his unborn child. Her only hope is that she would conceive. After all, if her plan failed, the pledge would be of little value. It would likely put her in danger with nothing but her word against his.

> What is the outcome of Tamar's single encounter with Judah, according to Genesis 38:18?

> Compare and contrast Tamar's actions with the actions of Onan, Judah's second son. What conclusions can you draw?

> God also has a staff (Exod. 4:20; Isa. 10:26), symbolizing not only His authority, but also His protection over His people.

> "Even though I walk through the valley of the shadow of death, I will fear no evil, for you are with me; your rod and your staff, they comfort me."
> —Psalm 23:4

Tamar's willingness to remain faithful to Judah's promise of Shelah, followed by her tenacious quest to continue Judah's family line, stands in stark contrast to the actions of Judah's son Onan. Even if Tamar's only motive was to secure a place in Judah's family, seeking to raise a family was an honorable aspiration for a woman in that day. Onan, however, refused to perpetuate the family line—an attitude that incurred the wrath of God and even cost him his life!

Trusting in God's Favor

Contrast the outcome of Tamar's single encounter with Judah with the time she spent married to Er and Onan. Do you think Tamar's encounter with Judah involved an act of faith on her part? Explain.

Read Genesis 20:18 and 29:31. What do these verses reveal about God's power over human conception?

Why do you think God withheld Tamar's ability to conceive with Er (and Onan, who deliberately sabotaged Tamar) but opened the way for her to conceive in her one encounter with Judah?

We are witnessing God's sovereignty at work in the story of Tamar. One commentator writes, "God sovereignly appoints the premature death of Judah's wife in order that Tamar's desire to continue the line of Judah might come to fruition."[12] Another writes, "Like the harlot Rahab, she seems to have had a knowledge of the promises made to Israel."[13] After all, Judah is a mere three generations from Abraham. God even promised Judah's father Jacob, "Kings shall come from your own body. The land that I gave to Abraham and Isaac I will give to you, and . . . to your offspring after you" (Gen. 35:11–12). Surely Tamar would have learned of Judah's family background, either before or during her marriages to Judah's sons. It was likely this blessing on Judah's family that young Tamar was clinging to. In so doing, whether she realized it or not, Tamar was placing her faith squarely on the promises of the one true God!

............................YOUR TURN............................

Think of a specific time when you held on tightly to God's promises. What was the outcome? What impact did it have on your faith?

In the margin, list each area of your life where you are clinging to God and His promises right now.

Day Four / Week Four

Are there any area(s) in your life right now where you need to hold on to God and His promises, but are struggling to do so? Explain.

Spend some time listening for God's voice, inviting Him to speak through His Word. If He places a scripture or thought on your heart, write it below.

DAY FIVE
Shifting the Balance of Power

In Day Three of this week's lesson, I briefly shared my regret over a particularly shameful season in my life. Unlike Judah, mine was far more than a one-time affair. Unlike Tamar, I was not trapped in circumstances with no way of escape. I cannot point my finger and say:

- It was his fault (or hers).
- I was a victim of my circumstances.
- I had no way out.

I was simply drowning in a sea of my own sin. Perhaps that is why it was so difficult for me to share. I have no excuse. I also know I am not alone. Maybe there is something in your past, or something you or a loved one is wrestling with right now, which you believe is too shameful for God to forgive, such as:

- a past abortion(s)
- a homosexual encounter or same-sex attraction
- an addiction, such as drugs, alcohol, or pornography
- involvement in the occult
- or _____ (you fill in the blank)

Whenever I think back on that particular sinful season of my life, my first reaction is to hang my head in shame, but I know that shame is not from God. On the other hand, if a past (or current) sin brings conviction leading to repentance, this is always from the Lord. In His kindness, He is drawing us to Himself, calling us to repent, surrender our sin, and enter His loving embrace of reconciliation.

> If a sin, once confessed and repented, again causes us to hide in shame, this is from the enemy—and we have to fight back.

But if a sin, once confessed and repented, again causes us to hide in shame, this is from the enemy, and we have to fight back. Whenever we are tempted to fall back into shame, we have a choice to make: Will we give in to the enemy's temptation, or will we fall to our knees and claim the truths from God's Word that our souls need to hear once again?

Read 1 John 1:9 below. Underline your responsibility, and circle each of God's promises.

> If we confess our sins, He is faithful and just to forgive us our sins and to cleanse us from all unrighteousness.

Once a sin is confessed, below are additional truths to claim whenever we are tempted to fall back into shame. Match each Scripture reference in the chart with the phrase that best describes it by drawing a line between each pair.

Revelation 7:9	I am cleansed of all sin by Christ's blood.
1 John 1:7	I am made new.
Ephesians 1:4	I am clothed in white.
Hebrews 10:22	I am cleansed from an evil conscience.
Romans 6:4	I am holy and blameless in God's sight.

Read each of the above truths at least once out loud. Which one speaks to your heart the most right now? Why?

> If you belong to Christ, God does not even see your sin! That's the power of Christ's redeeming blood.

God's Word assures us, "There is therefore now no condemnation for those who are in Christ Jesus" (Rom. 8:1). No condemnation. No means no, none, never. If you belong to Christ, God does not even *see* your sin! You can search for an eternity and will never find a single trace of condemnation or disappointment in His eyes. Instead, you will find yourself bathed in a sea of unending, holy love. That's the power of Christ's redeeming blood.

The Tide Begins to Turn

The following question is designed for discussion purposes. As the response calls for speculation, there are no right or wrong answers. Read Genesis 38:19.

As best you can, try to step into the mindset of a young woman living in that culture. During those first few days after Tamar's encounter with Judah, what do you suppose she may have been:

Thinking:

Feeling:

Hoping or praying:

It is certainly challenging for us to imagine ourselves in Tamar's sandals, living in that ancient culture. Added to that was her belief that her only way out of her situation was to prostitute herself to her father-in-law. While we do not know much about Tamar's personality through her story up to this point, we have discovered at least a few things about her. She was obedient, patient, resourceful, determined, and, some might even say, courageous.

Regardless of her strength of character and the culture, Tamar's experience with Judah would have been difficult to say the least. While we need to be careful not to interpret Tamar's experience through our cultural lens, we can only wonder what she was feeling those first few days. What thoughts went through her mind? Did she experience remorse? Shame? Disgust? Despair? When she laid down to sleep at night, did a voice whisper in her thoughts:

"You're a disgrace to your family."

"You're a *zona* and a sham."

"You might have had a chance to remarry before, but now look at what you've done. No one will want you now."

Or did she keep her mind and heart focused on her mission? Did she dream of the child she longed for? Did she trust that, in the end, Judah might do the right thing? Did she pray, perhaps even lift up a prayer to Judah's invisible God, daring to believe that He might bless her and give her success? We don't know the answers to these questions. However, we do know that God has been working out His plan of redemption since before time began, and for reasons we can never fully know this side of heaven, God chose Tamar to be an integral part of it.[14]

> "And we know that for those who love God all things work together for good, for those who are called according to his purpose." —Romans 8:28

Balance of Power

Prior to Tamar's encounter with Judah on the roadside, how would you view Tamar's position in life? Place an X on the line to indicate your response.

_____

powerless   secure

Explain.

How about Judah? Prior to his encounter with Tamar, how would you view Judah's position in life? Place an X on the line to indicate your response.

_____

powerless   secure

Explain.

PAUSE TO PONDER

> How about you? Underneath the loving protection of God's sovereignty, how do you see yourself at this point in your life? Place an X on the line to indicate your response.
>
> _____
>
> powerless   secure
>
> In what area of your life right now do you feel most powerless? In what area do you feel most secure and at peace? Take a few moments to give God praise for the peace and security you enjoy. At the same time, ask Him to help you see His sovereignty in the area(s) where you feel powerless.

Read Genesis 38:20. Why do you suppose Judah sent the young goat with his friend rather than going himself? List as many reasons as you can think of.

Glance back at Genesis 37:31-32. What similarities do you notice in this passage compared with the events in Genesis 38:20?

Over the past weeks, we have encountered a number of deceptions in this family drama. Compare Genesis 37:31-32 and Genesis 38:20 with Genesis 27:15-19. What object do all three stories share in common?

Do you suppose this is merely coincidence? Explain.

SUPPLEMENTAL READING

What's with All the Goats?

Having grown up "a city kid," I'll be the first to confess I don't know a lot about goats. Well, I didn't know much about goats, until I started writing this study. As I explored the stories leading up to Tamar, goats seemed to jump up all over the place (perhaps this isn't so surprising given their tendency to jump). First, it was Rebekah covering Jacob's hands with goat skins in order to deceive Isaac into thinking Jacob was his "hairy" brother Esau (in Hebrew, *goat* and *hairy* share the same root word). Next, it was Judah and his brothers dipping Joseph's coat in goat's blood to deceive their father. And then, in the story of Tamar, another goat! I began to wonder, what's with all the goats?

In my research, I learned a lot about goats. In biblical times, goats were highly prized for food, milk, and skins, and they were permitted by God for sacrifice (Lev. 16:7–10; Heb. 10:3–4). At the same time, keeping goats, even to this day, has its challenges. The animals are highly destructive. They do not just eat plants and grasses above the soil; left to themselves, they would eat every last living thing, right down to the roots. Although sheep and goats typically graze in the same areas, the animals often need to be separated due to the goats' aggressive disposition, making them a real danger to the sheep.[15]

In the Old Testament, "goat" sometimes symbolically represented demons, as in Leviticus 17:7, "They shall no more sacrifice their sacrifices to goat demons [literally, "goats"], after whom they whored" (see also 2 Chron. 11:15). Goats also represented oppressors and wicked men, as found in Ezekiel 34:17–22 and 39:18.[16] In the New Testament, goats are mentioned a number of times, perhaps most memorably by Jesus who, in speaking of the final judgment in Matthew 25:32, announces that, as King, "he will separate people one from another as a shepherd separates the sheep from the goats." The sheep represent believers who will enter God's kingdom; the goats, or unbelievers, represent those who will see eternal damnation. For the crowd listening to Jesus's words, this would have been a powerful visual. Today, specialized breeding has rendered sheep and goats distinguishable, but this was not the case in biblical times. The sheep and goats in Jesus's day shared so many physical features that they looked virtually identical, so much so that often only a shepherd could tell them apart.

As I was chasing goats along my biblical "rabbit trail," I learned something else. In addition to goats being highly destructive to land and a danger to the sheep with which they roam, there is another distinction between the animals, and it could not be more telling. If you want to know the difference between a goat and a sheep, you need only to see who is following whom. Goats go where they wish, and the goat herder follows behind. Sheep, on the other hand, follow their shepherd and listen for his voice.

Sending Another to Do Your Dirty Work

Glance again at Genesis 38:20. What was the outcome of Judah's friend's quest?

Read Genesis 38:21-22. (Note: due to differences in Bible translations,[17] in addition to your preferred Bible, read the passage in at least one of these Bible versions: English Standard Version, New American Standard Bible, or New International Version.) What three details does Judah's friend use to describe the missing woman, according to verse 21?

1.

2.

3.

Does anything strike you as odd? Explain. (Hint: compare verses 15 and 21.)

In Genesis 38:15, the original Hebrew text records that Judah assumed Tamar to be a *zona*; however, in verses 21–22, the Hebrew text records that Judah's friend was looking for a *qadesh*. It would seem that Judah provided his friend most, but not all, of the information he would need to find the woman.[18] Specifically, his friend was looking for a woman:

- at Enaim
- at the roadside
- who was a cult prostitute (or so Judah led his friend to believe)

What reason(s) might Judah have had for describing the mysterious woman to his friend as a *qadash* instead of a *zona*?

I confess. This part of the story has always intrigued me. As I prepared to study this passage more closely, I was eager to see if the words translated in verses 14 and 20–21 were simply due to the discretion of Bible translators—or if there was a difference in the original text. When I saw that the Hebrew words were most definitely distinct, I wondered why. Why did Judah want his friend to believe he visited with a cult prostitute over a street prostitute?

The answer lies in yet another deception. Even among pagans, visiting street prostitutes was looked down upon as immoral or at least as a shady behavior. To use the services of a cult prostitute, however, gave the impression that Judah was doing something religious. The Hebrew word for cult prostitute, *qadash*, is taken directly from the Hebrew root word *qodesh*, meaning holy or sacred in the sense of being set apart for religious purposes.

PAUSE TO PONDER

What comes to mind when you hear the word *holy*? In what way(s) have you observed what God considers holy transformed into something unholy in the name of religion? How might this grieve the heart of God?

Trusting in God's Favor

After his encounter with Tamar, rather than face his deeds, Judah sends his friend to do his dirty work. He tells his friend exactly where to find the woman, but he hides the fact that she is a *zona*. One commentator spells it out plainly: "when Judah uses the word [*qadash*], he is elevating the status of the woman he's looking for to that of a religious priestess and not something immoral—a prostitute. He does this to hide his shame."[19] In the meantime, Tamar returns home and quietly resumes her status as a widow. However, she does not return home empty-handed. She has Judah's signet and staff—a double pledge—and, unbeknownst to her, she would soon discover she is carrying Judah's child (in fact, two!).

At this point in the story, how would you view Tamar's position? Place an X on the line to indicate your response.

_____

powerless   secure

Explain.

How about Judah? At this point in the story, how would you view Judah's position? Place an X on the line to indicate your response.

_____

powerless   secure

Explain.

The girl who Judah readily sent back home has become a cunning young woman who is suddenly not so easy to find. It would seem that the balance of power is starting to shift.

........................YOUR TURN........................

How has your perception of Tamar evolved since you started this study?

If a friend asked you to describe what you have been learning through this study, what would you say?

Lesson Summary

What scripture, statement, or thought was most significant to you this week?*
Write it down, and then reword it into a prayer of response to God.

*Share your favorite takeaway with a friend or on social media using #TamarBibleStudy. A worship song that touches my heart and speaks beautifully to this week's lesson is "God Only Knows," by For King and Country.

Notes

[1] Jocelyn McWhirter, "Marriage," in *Lexham Bible Dictionary*, ed. John D. Barry et al. (Bellingham, WA: Lexham Press, 2016).

[2] We know that Shelah married at some point in time; his sons are listed in 1 Chronicles 4:21–22. Curiously, he named his firstborn Er.

[3] Yigal Tzadka, Orly Kihaly, and David Herman, eds., *Choice Words from the Story of Judah and Tamar* (Jerusalem: Good Times, n.d.), 13.

[4] The name can also mean "two fountains" since the Hebrew word *ayin* can also mean fountain or stream; however, the concept of "seeing" fits more readily based on the context of the narrative as a whole.

[5] Chad Brand et al., eds., *Holman Illustrated Bible Dictionary* (Nashville: Holman Bible Publishers, 2003), s.v. "Timnah."

[6] *ESV Study Bible* (Wheaton, IL: Crossway Bibles, 2008), 117.

[7] Tzadka, Kihaly, and Herman, *Choice Words*, 14.

[8] Carl Friedrich Keil and Franz Delitzsch, *Commentary on the Old Testament*, vol. 1 (Peabody, MA: Hendrickson, 1996), 219.

[9] Robert D. Bergen, "Genesis," in *CSB Study Bible: Notes*, ed. Edwin A. Blum and Trevin Wax (Nashville: Holman Bible Publishers, 2017), 66.

[10] This weakness becomes even more evident a few chapters later, in Judges 16, where Scripture records the famous story of Samson and Delilah.

[11] C. Van Dam, "Rod, Staff," in *Dictionary of the Old Testament: Pentateuch*, ed. T. Desmond Alexander and David W. Baker (Downers Grove, IL: InterVarsity Press, 2003), 693.

[12] Steven P. Carpenter, *The Story of Joseph and Judah: A Teacher's Narrative and Structural Commentary on Genesis 37–50* (Fort Lauderdale, FL: St. Andrews House, 2010), 26.

[13] John Peter Lange et al., *A Commentary on the Holy Scriptures: Genesis* (Bellingham, WA: Logos Bible Software, 2008), 593.

[14] See 2 Tim. 1:9 and Titus 1:2.

[15] Jack W. Vancil, "Goat, Goatherd," in *The Anchor Yale Bible Dictionary*, ed. David Noel Freedman (New York: Doubleday, 1992), 1,040.

[16] M. G. Easton, *Easton's Bible Dictionary* (New York: Harper & Brothers, 1893).

[17] The KJV and NKJV Bible translations use the English word *harlot* in both passages (Gen. 38:15, 20–21); however, the original Hebrew distinguishes the two types of prostitutes, which is difficult to discern in the KJV and NKJV versions.

[18] Another possibility is that Judah confided his actions to his friend but asked his friend not to reveal the whole truth.

[19] Tzadka, Kihaly, and Herman, *Choice Words*, 22.

Day Five / Week Four

NOTES

NOTES

PRAISING

FAITHFULNESS

SEVERAL MONTHS GO BY AFTER TAMAR DISAPPEARS WITH Judah's signet and staff. It seems that Judah goes on with life as usual until Tamar's pregnancy is exposed. Will this be Tamar's opportunity to finally vindicate herself? To show everyone who was really in the wrong?

As Tamar is being led to her fate, she makes her choice, and neither her life nor Judah's would ever be the same.

DAY ONE
When Your Reputation Is on the Line

In my experience, most people like to cook or bake, but not both. Me? I like to bake. (Good thing too, since I can't cook to save my life.) It's so easy to order a pizza delivered right to my door or pick up a delicious roasted chicken from the supermarket on the way home. But there is no substitute for a tray of hot-out-of-the-oven cookies or a freshly baked cake.

When it comes to baking, I learned one important lesson early on. I was fourteen years old and had set my sights on baking an impressive seven-layer cake. I didn't need any help, mind you; this was going to be a surprise for the whole family. I had everything ready: the cake pans, sugar, flour, butter, and eggs;

oh, and let's not forget the chocolate frosting! Using Mom's recipe book, I went to work. About ninety minutes later, my seven-layer cake was finished, all one and a half inches of it. It seems that I had overlooked one tiny but key ingredient: baking soda. Mom did her best not to laugh. My little brother (who, ironically, would one day graduate from the Culinary Institute of America) thought it was hysterical. Who knew that one misstep could cost so much?

Some missteps, like my baking fiasco, can be chalked up to inexperience. Few will result in long-term repercussions. But there are some mistakes that will change the trajectory of a person's life forever.

The Downward Spiral of Sin

Last week, we read that as Judah was heading home from Timnah, he saw a prostitute and turned to her at the roadside. Being tempted by something we see is one thing; choosing to move toward it is another. Judah had already made his first mistake. His willful wrong turn led to a wrong choice, which led to a fateful decision; he handed over his signet, cord, and staff—his veritable identity. Giving them to her as pledge for payment, he promised to send "a young goat from the flock" (v. 17).

> ### PAUSE TO PONDER
> Read James 1:14-15 in the margin. How have you seen this principle at work in your experience? How can you guard yourself against this dangerous downward spiral?

The fact that Judah sends the goat at all is a picture of contrasts. While retrieving his possessions is part of his motivation, he seems more concerned about fulfilling his promise of providing a goat to a roadside prostitute than fulfilling his obligation of providing a husband for his daughter-in-law.

How sad! And this is just one snapshot. It would seem that Judah had a history of sidestepping his obligations and refusing to face his crimes. Let's do a quick review.

For each scenario, fill in the blank with the missing word based on the events. I completed one for you.

When Judah and his brothers sold Joseph into slavery, they dipped Joseph's robe in goat's blood and _____ it back to their father (Gen. 37:32).

"But each person is tempted when he is lured and enticed by his own desire. Then desire when it has conceived gives birth to sin, and sin when it is fully grown brings forth death."

—James 1:14-15

After Judah's firstborn and second-born sons died, Judah <u>sent</u> Tamar back to her father's house under the pretense of waiting to marry Judah's youngest son once he was older (Gen. 38:11).

After Judah's encounter with Tamar, whom he presumed to be a prostitute, Judah had his friend _____ a young goat on his behalf in order to take back his signet and staff (Gen. 38:20).

Consider Judah's actions. What do you think would happen to a person who continuously sidesteps his obligations and refuses to face his crimes?

The Deception of Sin

Reread Genesis 38:20–22. Briefly summarize the events.

Read Genesis 38:23. What reason does Judah give for not taking further steps to attempt to find the woman and retrieve his possessions?

Contrast Judah's concern for his reputation with his concern for having his signet and staff restored to him. What conclusions can you draw?

How does Judah attempt to justify himself, according to the last half of Genesis 38:23?

Here we see a man whose behavior still leaves us shaking our heads. First, he thinks nothing of using a prostitute. Then, he thinks even less of surrendering his signet and staff. When the deed is done, instead of fulfilling his promise to

Praising God's Faithfulness

the woman himself, he looks around for someone else to use—in this case, to retrieve his property and save him from having to confront the woman, and his sin. We can only wonder if his signet and staff were not at risk whether he would have sent the goat at all.

Either way, in an attempt to appear religious, Judah lets his friend believe he had visited a cult prostitute. Finally, when the woman cannot be found, he goes so far as to justify himself, saying, "I sent this young goat" (v. 23). In other words, it's as if he is saying, "I did my part. It's not my fault she disappeared." When it comes down to retrieving his signet and staff or preserving his reputation, Judah chooses his reputation.

No guilt. No shame. No grasp of his sins. Judah is ready to simply move on and forget it ever happened.

> "The heart is deceitful above all things, and desperately sick; who can understand it?"
> —Jeremiah 17:9

PAUSE TO PONDER

Reflect on Jeremiah 17:9 in the margin. Was there ever a time when you were tempted to turn a blind eye to your sin? If so, what was the result? Did God intervene? If yes, how? If not, do you wish He had? Why or why not?

Judgment Takes an Unexpected Turn

Read Genesis 38:24.

This verse packs a punch! There is so much going on in this one verse. As such, we are going to tackle it slowly, breaking it down into segments. We will cover all but one of these segments today, leaving the last portion for tomorrow's lesson.

For each segment of Genesis 38:24 printed below, answer the questions that follow.

"About three months later": Consider all that has transpired up to this point; why would a span of three months be significant? (Hint: glance back at Genesis 38:18.)

"Judah was told, 'Tamar your daughter-in-law has been immoral. Moreover, she is pregnant by immorality.'"

Day One / Week Five

Glance back at Genesis 38:13. What parallel do you notice between this verse and Genesis 38:24?

What do Genesis 38:13 and 38:24 suggest about the community's concern and awareness of what is happening around them? In short, are Judah and Tamar's choices occurring in a vacuum—and why does it matter?

Consider your response to the previous question. What principle(s) can you apply to your own choices?

Let's pause here for a moment to do a brief Hebrew word study. The word used to describe the "crime" Tamar is accused of in Genesis 38:24 stems from the Hebrew root word *zanah*, which means to be a harlot or to engage in prostitution. This is the identical Hebrew root word for *zona*. Whether the person informing Judah believed that Tamar had literally prostituted herself (engaged in sex for payment) or had committed adultery apart from any financial arrangement made no difference. Either way, since Tamar was still considered pledged to Judah's son Shelah, Tamar would be condemned for her unfaithfulness.

Contrast the consequences Judah expected to face if his actions were discovered (Gen. 38:23) with the consequences Tamar was willing to risk for her actions.

Why do you suppose Tamar was willing to risk so much? List as many reasons as you can think of.

It's no coincidence that knowledge of Tamar's pregnancy was revealed about three months later. During those first few months, few would have suspected Tamar could be pregnant. As far as anyone knew, she was still a widow. While it's possible that someone discovered Tamar's secret, it may have been Tamar herself who decided it was time to make her pregnancy known.

As a matter of fact, a woman hoping to conceive will often wait three months before making the news of pregnancy public. This typically occurs for two reasons. Not only will the woman have confidence that she indeed had conceived after missing three cycles, but the first three months of pregnancy also carry the highest risk of miscarriage. If Tamar wanted to reveal the news of her pregnancy, waiting three months makes perfect sense.

But there is something else in the narrative that seems peculiar. We read that Judah *was told* the news of Tamar's pregnancy. This wording is identical to the wording we examined last week when Tamar *was told* about Judah's activity in Genesis 38:13. Both verses use the same verb: *yug-gad*. The passive form of the verb suggests that something underhanded is happening, and from Judah's perspective, if anything fit that category, it would be the shocking news of Tamar's pregnancy.

We also read that the person who spoke to Judah referred to Tamar as his daughter-in-law. This is another parallel with verse 13. We can only wonder if Tamar herself arranged this person's covert mission to inform Judah of her condition, or at least, if Tamar purposely allowed her pregnancy to become known, confident that the news would quickly reach Judah's ears. Either way, the reference to Tamar as his daughter-in-law would remind Judah that Tamar was still under his authority. She was still considered a part of his family, even if he had sent her back to wait at her father's house. It is this aspect of Tamar's position that enables Judah to command her fate.

Next to each question, circle either "yes" or "no." When Judah was told about Tamar, did he:

Ask the messenger any questions?	Yes	No
Consult Tamar's father?	Yes	No
Confront Tamar?	Yes	No
Consult the village elders?	Yes	No
Hesitate to pronounce judgment?	Yes	No
Extend mercy, such as divorcing her from Shelah?	Yes	No

Day One / Week Five

Contrast Judah's response to Tamar's "crimes" with his attitude toward his own actions in Genesis 38:20 and 38:23. How might this grieve God's heart?

Read Matthew 7:1-2 and Romans 2:3. What warnings do these verses convey?

By this time, Judah would have been more than forty years old, yet he is still blind to his own sin and hypocrisy. Sadly, some people can live their entire lives quick to point out the sin of others while refusing to recognize the guilty face in the mirror. But God is merciful, and Judah could never have imagined whom God would use to open his eyes.

YOUR TURN

Why do you think it's easier for us to judge another person's sin than it is to recognize that same sin in ourselves?

Spend some time in prayer, asking God to reveal any "blind spots" to your own sin that He wishes for you to recognize. Write a prayer of confession as He leads you.

If nothing comes to mind at this time, take a few moments to thank God for how He has exposed "blind spots" in your past, leading you to repentance. Write a prayer of gratitude.

> Do you suppose, O man—you who judge those who practice such things and yet do them yourself—that you will escape the judgment of God?
> —Romans 2:3

DAY TWO
Choosing the High Road

Yesterday, we ended our lesson with the realization that Judah was still oblivious to his own sin. In fact, he was living a double standard. He had no problem using the services of a prostitute, but when he was told Tamar prostituted herself, he was quick to condemn her. Sadly, his mindset was simply a reflection of society at the time. Roughly 1,600 years later, little had changed. Let's skip ahead briefly to the New Testament and take a look.

Casting the First Stone

Among the more well-known stories in the New Testament is the story of the woman caught in adultery. Jesus is sitting at the center of a crowd of people who gathered to listen to His teaching. All of a sudden, a group of religious leaders drag a distraught woman through the crowd and make her stand in front of Jesus. The story appears in John 8.

> Read John 8:3-7. Compare these events with those we have been studying in Genesis 38 (most notably verses 15-16 and 24). In the space below, list three or four similarities and differences that stand out to you. I completed one of each to help you get started.

Similarities	Differences
A woman is accused of immorality.	In John 8, there is no indication of prostitution or payment involved.

While the circumstances surrounding these stories are different, the similarities are noteworthy. Both women are subjected to public humiliation, while the men are nowhere to be found. A death sentence is quickly pronounced. In John 8, we are told right from the start that the purpose of the accusation was an attempt to trap Jesus, but Jesus turns the tables on His accusers, forcing them to face their own sin and hypocrisy.

In the same way, the tables are about to turn on Judah.

"And Judah said, 'Bring her out, and let her be burned'" (Gen. 38:24). Though Judah was not yet aware of his role in Tamar's pregnancy, why do you suppose he was so quick to demand the death sentence? List as many reasons as you can think of.

Of the reasons you listed, which stands out to you the most? Why?

Not only does Judah fail to recognize his own hypocrisy, but his pronouncement is so swift, we can only wonder if he felt relieved for his sudden good fortune of having a way to be rid of the girl once and for all. His judgment, "let her be burned," (v. 24) goes beyond the cultural norm of that time. More often, the punishment for adultery would be death by stoning (if the one having the authority chose to demand the sentence). Even in this Gentile region, from the community's standpoint, Judah would appear to be the one in the right at this point. His daughter-in-law had been unfaithful, and it was within Judah's right to demand she pay for her crime.

Nevertheless, Judah had the choice of extending at least some measure of mercy to the girl, such as issuing a certificate of divorce. After all, a divorce would have just as easily freed him from his dilemma of withholding his son Shelah. Did he not carry even a sliver of guilt as one who used prostitutes himself? And what about the life in Tamar's womb? Does his conscience not bother him at all? Apparently not—he asks no questions; he extends no mercy. In fact, he demands that the girl suffer even more than stoning: "Let her be burned."

PAUSE TO PONDER

> Think of a time when it was within your power to choose whether to extend mercy or to demand justice for a wrong you suffered. What did you do and why? Next, think of a time when a person extended mercy to you instead of judgment. Why do you suppose they responded as they did? How did their decision impact you?

. Praising God's Faithfulness

Although God's law had not been written at the time of these events and Judah was living in a pagan land, the circumstances where the Bible demands an adulterer to be burned with fire are intriguing. It occurs in only two situations: if a man marries both a woman and the woman's mother (Lev. 20:14) and if the daughter of God's priest commits adultery (Lev. 21:9).

It is interesting that Judah lets his friend Hirah believe he had used the services of a pagan priestess (cult prostitute) and is now demanding a punishment that would one day be reserved for immoral daughters of God's priests. Judah, feigning righteous indignation, demands that his daughter-in-law be burned for her immorality. This, coming from the man who allowed his daughter-in-law to be abused and used by his sons, then cast out altogether when Judah denied her rights in accordance with levirate practice. If Judah only knew that he was about to come face-to-face with his own hypocrisy.

Surrendering Your Fate

Read Genesis 38:25.

Like the verse before it, this verse is loaded with action. As we did for verse 24, we are going to tackle verse 25 slowly, breaking it down into segments. We will cover all but the last of these segments today, leaving the final portion for tomorrow's lesson.

For each segment of Genesis 38:25 printed below, answer the questions that follow.

"As she was being brought out": in addition to studying what is written in a passage, at times we can further our understanding by pondering what is omitted; does Scripture record anyone coming to Tamar's defense?

Imagine you are Tamar. With no one coming to your aid, what might you be doing?

Pause here a few moments, and picture the events in your mind. Below I've listed various people who were (or likely were) at the scene. Slowly ponder each one and their role in the events; try to imagine what they might have been doing, thinking, or feeling. Choose at least three from the list; next to each of the three, record your thoughts.

The men leading Tamar to her death

The messenger Tamar sends to Judah

The crowd of people watching the procession

The public executioners

Judah

Judah's friend Hirah

Judah's son Shelah

Tamar's father

Tamar's other family and friends

Record your thoughts next to each of the other person(s) listed above, in addition to the three you already completed.

Of the people listed in the previous exercise, apart from Tamar and Judah, which person or group captures your interest the most? Why?

If this were a movie, these events would provide a dramatic moment. Even in that time and culture, it was not every day that someone was sentenced to death, much less by fire. Clearly, Judah held a lot of authority. No sooner does he pronounce judgment than we are told Tamar is being led to her fate.

Whether it happened immediately, a few hours later, or a date was set, someone would be preparing for the execution. Wood would be gathered. A stake would be set in place. The procession begins to form as Tamar is led through the crowd. But perhaps she is ready; perhaps she has spent the past three months preparing for this very day. As she is taken away, she clings tightly onto a long narrow object wrapped securely in a cloth along with a smaller object clutched in her other hand. With all the courage she can muster, she releases the objects into the hand of a messenger who quickly brings them to Judah.

Praising God's Faithfulness

"As she was being brought out, she sent word to her father-in-law, 'By the man to whom these belong, I am pregnant.'" Tamar took a risk by secretly sending a messenger to Judah with the staff and seal. Do you find Tamar's actions surprising? Unwise? Disappointing? Share your thoughts.

List everything you can think of that could have gone wrong for Tamar.

Of the list you made, which one stands out to you the most? Why?

> "For the LORD will vindicate his people and have compassion on his servants."
> —Psalm 135:14

Talk about the ninth hour! If we were watching this scene play out on a movie screen, we would be gripping the edges of our seats right about now. After all, Tamar has placed her only hope of redemption squarely in her executioner's hands. She surrenders her one and only bargaining chip. Talk about faith! Talk about courage! She is literally walking to her execution, and she makes no public defense. She points no blame. She does not even remind Judah of his betrayal, and she allows the community to believe *she* was the betrayer. Sparing Judah public humiliation, she places her life—and the life in her womb—fully in her betrayer's hands.

PAUSE TO PONDER

> If your fate were held in the hands of the person who betrayed you, what would it take for you to choose to surrender your only hope of vindication?

I sometimes have to remind myself that these are real events experienced by real people. At the same time, I am deeply encouraged in knowing that above it all is a sovereign God watching over the children of man. From the beginning, He has been at work *behind the seen*, fulfilling His wonderful purposes within human history, most of which we will never fully understand this side of heaven (and much of which will forever be known only to the mind of God.)

Recall from Week One: What is God looking for? Fill in the blanks in the sentence below. (Hint: see the beginning of Day Four of Week One.)

God has been working *behind the seen* throughout the generations of man, seeking to _____ _____ a people for Himself.

From Seth to Noah, then to Abraham, Isaac, and Jacob—as we journey through the story of Judah and Tamar, it is encouraging to see that God does not always choose the people who get everything right (if He did, there would be no one to choose!). Instead, He sometimes chooses those who seem to get everything wrong but are willing to learn from their mistakes. There are even times when He chooses those who don't seem to learn (like the prophet Jonah). At the end of the day, these events simply remind us that "God chooses whom he chooses."[1]

................................YOUR TURN................................

Think of someone God chose to accomplish His wonderful purposes that leaves you shaking your head wondering "Why? Why did God choose *that* person?" The person can be someone in the Bible, someone you have read about, or someone you know personally.

Why does God's choice surprise you?

If it were up to you, what would you have done differently?

How about your life? Is there anything about your life that you believe (or previously believed) prevents God from choosing you to accomplish His wonderful purposes? Explain.

Take a few moments and give God praise for His willingness to choose people like Judah and Tamar—and ordinary people like you and me—to accomplish His wonderful purposes.

> God sometimes chooses those who seem to get everything wrong but are willing to learn from their mistakes.

Day Three
Waiting for Your Vindication

During my teenage years, I lived with my family in upstate New York. The country road that led to our home intersected a railroad crossing. Because vehicular traffic was light on the roads and the freight trains were infrequent, there was no crossing gate installed. Rather, when a train was approaching, the red lights would flash as the train sounded its horn in the distance. The freight trains that traveled the tracks were often long, which tried the patience of my younger brother and me as we waited with Mom in the car, idling at a safe distance. To keep us distracted, Mom would challenge us to count all of the cargo cars. I think our all-time record was close to 150.

When I turned sixteen years old, I couldn't wait to get my driver's permit. One Sunday afternoon, my mom and stepdad came with me in the car so I could practice driving. We stayed on the back roads, which were less traveled. Though I can chuckle about it now, there was one day in particular that I will never forget. Before I tell you the story, I need to share a little bit about my parents' personalities. My mom is free-spirited and more of a risk-taker than my stepdad. In that regard, they are about as opposite as can be. My stepdad is careful and detailed and tends to be on the quieter side. I love them both, but having them together in the car with me that day was, well, I'm glad my driving instructor wasn't in the car with us.

I was driving along the back roads, getting used to the car and feel of the pedals beneath my feet. As we neared a familiar bend in the road, my mom saw it first. A train was approaching in the distance as I approached the railroad tracks. Although I had several moments to decide whether to speed up or slow down, I was inexperienced and wasn't sure what to do. Simultaneously, my mom blurted out, "Hurry up! You can make it!" while my stepdad in the back seat commanded, "Slow down! You need to stop!"

Both feet reacted at once—one hit the brake and the other hit the gas. The car jerked forward, the tires screeched, and I hit the brake a second time, finally coming to a stop just short of the tracks as the train barreled by. I'll never forget the incredulous look on my stepdad's face in the rearview mirror as he silently reprimanded my mother. Poor Mom. Had I not hesitated, there was plenty of time to get across. Either way, that was probably not the best lesson in this young driver's training.

Day Three / Week Five

Two Voices, Two Directions

Throughout our lives, whether we recognize it or not, two voices are vying for our attention, each one urging us in the opposite direction of the other. In time, we learn to drown out the voice we prefer not to hear, unwittingly giving power and strength to the other. Judah had been listening to one voice for a long time, and it wasn't until he came face-to-face with the consequences of his choices that his ears—and eyes—were finally opened. Let's take a look.

> "And she said, 'Please identify whose these are, the signet and the cord and the staff.' Then Judah identified them . . ." (Gen. 38:25–26). As Judah considered the objects presented to him, he had a number of choices. List as many options as you can think of.

Curiously, it is this point in the story that echoes events that occurred one chapter before. Glance back at Genesis 37:31–33. Listed in the table are several aspects of Tamar's story. Place an X in the center column next to each circumstance if it also appears in the story of Joseph.

	True for Joseph's Story	True for Tamar's Story
One-of-a-kind personal item(s) were sent to father/father-in-law		X
The items were sent by way of a messenger		X
Father/father-in-law identifies the personal item(s)		X

Read Genesis 38:26. Do you think the events in Genesis 37 may have played a part in Judah's sudden turnaround? Explain.

What else contributed to Judah's change of heart, according to Genesis 38:26?

Praising God's Faithfulness

Which tactics did Tamar use to achieve her goal of conceiving a child and securing a place in Judah's family? Circle all that apply.

prostitution   deception   secrecy

✒ Since both Judah and Tamar were guilty of all the above, how could Judah declare that Tamar is "more righteous" than himself?

These events can be challenging for us to understand. You and I live in a world far from that culture, time, and place. Tamar may have acted deceitfully, but as one commentary author explains, "it was within her rights; she did nothing that the law did not entitle her to do."[2] Tamar had every right to bear a child for Judah's line. In light of Judah's rebellion against God by marrying a Canaanite, followed by God's judgment on his two wicked sons and Judah's withholding Shelah from marriage to Tamar, he was well on his way to destroying his family line altogether. Not only that, but Judah's actions were a direct affront to God's promise to bless and multiply the family line of Abraham, Isaac, and Jacob.

One scholar writes, "Tamar is one of those foreigners . . . who put the descendants of Abraham to shame by being more concerned with righteousness and the fulfillment of God's purposes than the chosen line."[3] That is a remarkable contrast, given the fact that Scripture does not come right out and tell us the thoughts or motivations behind Tamar's actions. However, a careful examination of the context can often shed some light on the places where Scripture is otherwise silent. Let's pause here a moment and review what we have learned up to this point.

The Call of God

We have traced the genealogy from Adam to Seth to Noah, to Abraham, Isaac, and Jacob. Along the way, we have witnessed God's righteous anger against wickedness, His loving protection over His creation, including Noah and his family during the flood, and His faithful covenant with Abraham, Isaac, and Jacob. God's plan to bring a Savior into the world has been unfolding since the beginning, and while rebellion and sin would seem to get in the way at every turn, God's plan cannot be thwarted. For reasons known only in the mind of God, He chose Judah and Tamar to be a part of that plan.

On the chart on page 247, cross out the name of Jacob's firstborn, Reuben, and write the name Judah above "Jacob."[4]

Day Three / Week Five

Read 2 Timothy 1:9 in the margin. What comes to mind when you hear "holy calling"? How would you define it?

> "[God] saved us and called us to a holy calling, not because of our works but because of his own purpose and grace."
> —2 Timothy 1:9

Read 1 Peter 5:10 and Philippians 3:14 and 20. Compare these verses with your above response. Are they the same or different? Explain.

Which comes first? God's call to set us apart or the manner in which we live our lives and serve His purposes?

Why does it matter?

For Christians, our calling is not so much what we do for God as it is sometimes understood; instead, it is living in the light of the glorious hope of salvation we have in Him. What is true today was the same in ancient times. To be called by God is the simple but profound blessing of being set apart by Him and for Him. Just as Judah would seem an unlikely choice, God also chose Tamar, even though on the outside it would appear she had every strike against her. She was (presumably) Canaanite. She purposely set out to deceive Judah and was willing to prostitute herself. Despite her questionable methods, beneath it all was a heart that beat in sync with God's will. She clung fiercely to her desire to bear a son for Judah's family. To that end, she suffered silently, she waited patiently, and only after learning of Judah's betrayal and the news of his wife's passing did she shed her widow's garb and assert her rights. In the end, it would seem that God answered her prayer: ". . . and she conceived" (Gen. 38:18).

> God is looking for hearts that beat in sync with His will.

Three months later, Judah is confronted with his sin. Rather than accusing Tamar of stealing his seal and staff, or finding some other way of shifting the blame, he finally reaches the end of himself, acknowledging, "She is more righteous than I." It is here where we get another glimpse of God at work *behind the seen*: that He would use a faithful Canaanite girl to bring about the humble confession

of a rebellious son of Israel is a picture of God's grace and mercy, as well as His mysterious ways.

PAUSE TO PONDER

> What comes to mind when you hear the word *righteous*? By what means does Scripture define a person as righteous, according to 2 Corinthians 5:21? As a Christian, do you struggle (or have you struggled) with the idea that God declares you righteous? Explain.

Read the verses listed, and complete the table.

Reference	What is promised?	To whom is it promised?
Proverbs 10:24b		
Proverbs 15:29b		
Psalm 34:19		
James 5:16b		

Of the promises you listed, which one do you need from God today? Rewrite the verse into a prayer.

> "The prayer of a righteous person is powerful and effective."
> —James 5:16b NIV

The promises in the prior verses are wonderful, but there may be times when you and I find it difficult to embrace the idea that God considers us righteous. After all, we know that we fail—every day! Praise God that our righteousness is not dependent on us, *but on Him* (Rom. 5:19; see also Rom. 3:21–22).

The Turning Point

What is true today was true then. Judah's words declaring Tamar "more righteous" are one thing, but then we get a glimpse into the first sign of Judah's true transformation: "And he did not know her again" (Gen. 38:26). This "knowing" is in the intimate sense. I confess that when I first began to study the story, this summary statement felt a bit abrupt. I don't know about you, but I want to know more. After all, the next segment of the story (which we will begin exploring tomorrow) begins with Tamar going into labor. Between Tamar being dragged to the execution site and the account of her giving birth, all we read is Judah's confession and the fact that "he did not know her again."

While I was curious to know more, nothing of importance is missing. The last words of Genesis 38:26 mark a beautiful turning point for both Judah and Tamar. Judah, no longer driven by his lusts and selfishness, takes Tamar into his home as her provider and protector, but he never again allows her to be humiliated or used. For Tamar, instead of shame and death, her reputation is vindicated, as new life fills her womb and her future.

YOUR TURN

*And Abraham "believed the LORD,
and he counted it to him as righteousness."*

Genesis 15:6

What is the relationship between faith and righteousness, according to Genesis 15:6?

Consider 2 Corinthians 5:21 in the margin. Earlier, I asked if you struggle (or have struggled) with the idea that God declares you righteous. Take a few moments in prayer, and ask God to reveal if there is anything you are trying to do to earn His favor. Record what He reveals.

> "For our sake [God] made [Christ] to be sin who knew no sin, so that in him we might become the righteousness of God."
>
> —2 Cor. 5:21

DAY FOUR
Stepping Out in Faith

We have certainly covered a lot of material these past weeks. Take a few moments right now to appreciate how hard you have worked and how far you have come. Please know I am praying for you and cheering you on as you press forward through Tamar's story.

At the end of Week Three, we took some time to examine the simple outline of Genesis 38. The chapter is divided into three time segments, each one more condensed than the last. Over the past weeks of our study, we covered the first two time segments, verses 1–26. Today we will dive into the details of the final segment of our story. The author devotes close to one-sixth of the chapter to this last segment. At the same time, if we were to map it out, the events in this last segment span an infinitesimal percentage of the chapter's timeline, attesting to their significance in the story.

Fighting for First Place

Read Genesis 38:27–30 to get an overview of the passage. What is the first thing we are told concerning Tamar's pregnancy, according to verse 27?

Glance back at the events surrounding another pregnancy two generations earlier by reading Genesis 25:22. What is the first thing recorded concerning Rebekah's pregnancy? Fill in the missing word: *The children _____ together within her.*

Now read Genesis 25:24–26. Compare and contrast this birth event with Tamar's in Genesis 38:27–30. What similarities do you notice?

In addition to the strange details of the twins' behavior during their birth in both accounts, Genesis 38:27 is written nearly verbatim to Genesis 25:24. It seems that the writer wants to remind us of the earlier struggle. Just like Rebekah's two generations prior, here is another remarkable twin birth. Even though the birth of twins would usually be considered a divine blessing or approval,[5] within each generation of God's chosen line, we witness some kind of conflict, one that often centers on the issue of being firstborn. In short, nothing is easy for God's people. The fact that either woman survived such a high-risk pregnancy in that day is evidence of God's divine protection.

Reread Genesis 38:27–28. Briefly describe the events.

Based on the actions of the midwife, how significant was identifying the firstborn in that culture? Place an X on the line to indicate your response.

_____
not significant   highly significant

In biblical times, what would every firstborn son expect to receive in relation to that title? Circle all that apply. (Hint: refer back to p. 44.)

    special garment

    double portion of the inheritance

    honor

    his choice of a wife

    to become the family's next leader

God doesn't always see things the way we do. To the surprise of many of the Bible's patriarchs, God often bypassed the firstborn son in favor of another. For example, when God did not choose Abraham's firstborn son Ishmael[6] but passed the covenant promises on to Isaac, Abraham was deeply distressed (Gen. 17:18). In a similar fashion, rather than choosing Isaac's firstborn son Esau, God allowed Jacob's disguise and Isaac's failing eyesight to deceive him into blessing Esau's twin brother Jacob instead (Gen. 35:11–12).

Nevertheless, the expected privileges of the firstborn continued in that culture through the generations. In addition to receiving a double portion of the inheritance, as well as the privilege of assuming his father's authority as leader of the family after his father's death, to possess the title of firstborn son was considered a high honor.[7] Therefore, it is no surprise that when it came time for Tamar to give birth, the midwife, despite all her responsibilities and tasks, would take the necessary measures to ensure that the firstborn son would be clearly identified.

Why a Scarlet Thread?

Mentioning the tying of the thread (which was likely nearby in order to tie off the umbilical cord) is one thing, but it is interesting that Scripture also records the color of the thread. After all, why does it matter what color it was? Why would this detail be included unless it has some significance? It turns out that not only is this the first mention of a scarlet thread in the Bible, but it is mentioned in Tamar's story not once, but twice.

On the surface, this may not seem such a big deal. After all, later on, the use of scarlet thread or fabric occurs frequently in the Bible. It occurs repeatedly in

> "The LORD sees not as man sees: man looks on the outward appearance, but the LORD looks on the heart." —1 Samuel 16:7

relation to the construction of the tabernacle (2 Chron. 2), and it is used to symbolize royalty (Matt. 27:28) as well as luxury or prosperity (e.g., 2 Sam. 1:24 and Rev. 18:16). However, the color scarlet is also associated with blood, purification laws, and sin (as found in Num. 19:1–9 and Heb. 9:19–22). Not only that, but concerning the events in Genesis 38, we again see a struggle as to who the firstborn is. The scarlet thread foreshadows God's plan of redemption through the blood of Jesus, who is "the firstborn among many brothers" (Rom. 8:29).

Read Hebrews 9:22 and Isaiah 1:18 in the margin. Why does God describe sin in terms of the color scarlet?

> "Come now, let us reason together, says the LORD: though your sins are like scarlet, they shall be as white as snow."
> —Isaiah 1:18

Scripture paints a sober picture of God's view of sin, but praise His name for the hope of redemption! And this hope—first illustrated by a simple scarlet thread—is beautifully captured in another Old Testament story of another scarlet strand. Perhaps you are familiar with the story of Rahab, or maybe you will enjoy learning about her today for the first time. It requires some extra reading, but I promise it will be worth it.

Read the following passage from Joshua 2. Underline at least two keywords or phrases that are also prominent in Tamar's story.

And Joshua . . . sent two men . . . as spies, saying, "Go, view the land, especially Jericho." And they went and came into the house of a prostitute whose name was Rahab and lodged there. . . . she had brought them up to the roof and hid them [from the king's messengers . . . and Rahab said] "I know that the LORD has given you the land . . . for the LORD your God, he is God in the heavens above and on the earth beneath. Now then, please swear to me by the LORD that, as I have dealt kindly with you, you also will deal kindly with my father's house, and give me a sure sign that you will . . . deliver [my family] from death." . . . The men said to her, ". . . Behold, when we come into the land, you shall tie this scarlet cord in the window through which you let us down, and you shall gather into your house . . . all your father's household. . . ." And she said, "According to your words, so be it." . . . And she tied the scarlet cord in the window. (Josh. 2:1–21, selected)

How are the motivations of Tamar and Rahab similar? What are they each hoping for?

PAUSE TO PONDER

> How about you? What deep desire are you holding on to in this season of your life? Is there a lesson you have gleaned from Tamar's experience that you could apply to your situation?

Next, read the following passages from Joshua 6 and Matthew 1.

And the LORD said to Joshua, "See, I have given Jericho into your hand. . . . Joshua said to the people, "Shout, for the LORD has given you the city. And the city and all that is within it shall be devoted to the LORD for destruction. Only Rahab the prostitute and all who are with her in her house shall live, because she hid the messengers whom we sent. . . . Rahab the prostitute and . . . all who belonged to her, Joshua saved alive. And she has lived in Israel to this day. (Josh. 6:2–25, selected)

The book of the genealogy of Jesus Christ, the son of David, the son of Abraham. Abraham was the father of Isaac . . . and Judah the father of Perez and Zerah by Tamar . . . and Salmon the father of Boaz by Rahab. (Matt. 1:1–5, selected)

What else do Rahab and Tamar share in common, according to Matthew 1?

Which aspect of each woman's story stirs your heart the most?

Rahab:

Tamar:

Praising God's Faithfulness

Finally, what do their stories reveal about God's heart?

Courageous Steps of Faith

I love how God's Word is so interconnected. That's why it is easy to get caught up in "rabbit trails"—side stories and fascinating insights that may lead us far from where we originally started. However, in God's story, even rabbit trails are not without their reward. In the story of God's destruction of the wicked city of Jericho, we see the beautiful picture of God taking notice of one foreign woman—a prostitute no less—who acknowledged His sovereignty and aided His people. Because she protected the two Israelite spies, they gave her a sign—a scarlet cord—promising to deliver not only her, but her entire family.

In the same way, God blessed Tamar, a Canaanite girl willing to disguise herself as a prostitute in order to save not only herself but Judah's future family line. Both women sought a place among God's people. They may not have understood everything about Israel's God, but they each took courageous steps of faith. In the end, God graciously grafted each one into His covenant nation. More than that, He etched their names in His eternal Word as women He chose to weave into the lineage of Christ, the Savior of the world.

What symbolism is at work in the stories of Rahab and Tamar? What does the scarlet cord ultimately point to?

> We may not understand all that God is doing, but He takes notice when we are willing to step out in faith.

Read Genesis 38:28-30.

Which twin did the midwife declare came out first?

Which twin came out first?

Do you suppose these events could have been a source of conflict in the brothers' future? Explain.

Day Four / Week Five

The name Perez means *breach*. Look up *breach* in a dictionary. In what way(s) does the birth of Perez seem a fitting picture of Tamar's own struggle?

In what way(s) does the birth of Perez (and Zerah) reveal God's blessing on Tamar? Describe all the ways Tamar's life would have changed.

How about Judah? In what way(s) would the birth of Perez and Zerah have been a blessing for Judah?

This is a beautiful picture of redemption. Whereas Tamar had lived as a childless widow—even resorting to prostitution—she is now under the protection of Judah, and her arms are filled with the joy of children. And then there is Judah. Having lost his firstborn and secondborn sons, then widowed, God restores to him not one but two sons at the same time! What a merciful God! Despite all of Judah's faults and failures, God is quick to forgive and restore when Judah reaches the point of repentance. And Tamar, despite her suffering and questionable choices, remained faithful to her commitment to continue Judah's family line, a commitment that God saw fit to reward.

YOUR TURN

Describe one way you are encouraged by Tamar, her story, or God's activity in her life *behind the seen*.

Although Tamar may have known little about God, by His grace, she was grafted into God's covenant family. Scripture teaches that God "desires all people to be saved and to come to the knowledge of the truth" (1 Tim. 2:4). Perhaps you have never made the decision to receive God's gift of salvation and forgiveness of your sins. If that is the case, you can respond to His marvelous gift right now.

Praising God's Faithfulness

God promises in His Word that "In [Jesus] we have redemption through his blood, the forgiveness of our trespasses, according to the riches of his grace" (Eph. 1:7).

If you are ready to follow Jesus as the Lord and Savior of your life, go to God right now in prayer and confess your sin of living your life apart from Him. Thank Him for sending His son Jesus who died on the cross for your sin and then rose to life again. Commit to living for Him from this day forward. Write your prayer in the margin, with today's date. Then share your news with a friend, a group leader, or another member of the study. They'll be thrilled!

If you have previously accepted God's gift of salvation, made possible only through the death and resurrection of Jesus Christ, record the time and circumstances surrounding your experience in the margin. Follow it with a prayer of thanksgiving to God for His boundless love and faithfulness.

If you sense you need more time, ask God to bless your commitment to reading His Word and to help you be sensitive to His voice as you continue through this study.

Day Five
Embracing a New Identity

I love studying God's Word, don't you? It seems that no matter how far down we dig, there is always more to discover. Even the names of people and places can shed light on the text. In Genesis 38, not only did we gain insights from Judah and Er's names, but the names of the towns where the events took place have meaning as well. Let's do a quick review.

Match each name with the word(s) that are associated with the name. I included a few hints if you need them. I also completed one for you.

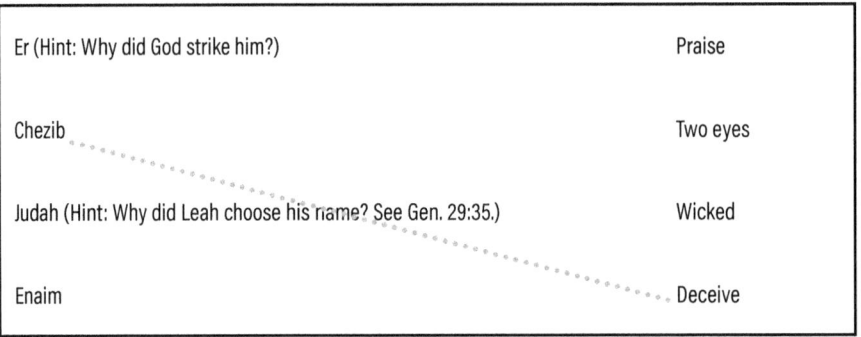

🌿 Consider the events of Genesis 38. Briefly describe how each place name figuratively plays into the events in the story.

Chezib:

Enaim:

What's in a Name?

With so many insights associated with the names of people and places in Genesis 38, it seems only fitting that Tamar's name would likewise add richness to the story.

Recall from Week Two the meaning of Tamar's name: _____ _____.
(Hint: glance back at page 83.)

Read Psalm 92:12-13 in the margin. What kind of people are associated with the meaning of Tamar's name?

> "The righteous flourish like the palm tree.... They are planted in the house of the Lord." —Psalm 92:12-13

Throughout Scripture, particularly in Psalms and Proverbs, the writers distinguish the "righteous" from the "wicked," such as in Proverbs 15:29: "The Lord is far from the wicked, but he hears the prayer of the righteous." While God alone is wholly righteous, those whom He calls to Himself slowly learn to walk in righteousness. They may stumble at first and fail at various times, but because they belong to Him, the Bible describes them as "righteous."

In Genesis 38, not only is Tamar acknowledged as "more righteous," but she is the only woman in the chapter identified by name. As we discovered in Week Two, Scripture provides a stark contrast between how Tamar and Judah's wife are introduced in the narrative. While we know Judah's wife was Canaanite, we are

Praising God's Faithfulness

never told her name. However, Scripture introduces us to Tamar by name, but her nationality (which was likely Canaanite) is never mentioned.

A careful look at the structure of Genesis 38 further reveals the contrast between the two women. The death of Judah's wife serves as a turning point in the narrative because, from that point forward, things begin to shift from misery and death to hope and life. Although Judah continues to make poor choices, God blesses Tamar with conception as she clings to her desire to be identified with Judah's family. One commentary author explains that it is here where "God reverses the flow of Judah's life and fortunes among the Canaanites by making Tamar a source of life and blessing to Judah, and the one used to awaken Judah to his covenantal responsibilities and restore him to his family."[8]

Beauty Hidden Within

This remarkable turn of events is beautifully depicted in the structure of the text itself. Examining a text's structure can seem tedious, but when we take the time to do so, we will gain marvelous insights into God's Word that are difficult to see otherwise. Admittedly, the structure of Genesis 38 is somewhat complex. Scholars have proposed a variety of outlines in an effort to organize its multiple layers, chiasms (I will explain *chiasm* shortly), and parallels. As we journeyed through the chapter, we often noted various parallels and connections—not only within the chapter itself, but also relating to the events in Genesis 37, as well as the stories of Samson and Rahab. However, for our purposes, we are going to keep it fairly simple by focusing on the general overview of the story. In fact, we have already done much of the work by identifying the three "time" segments in the chapter, which serve as the broad outline.

In Scripture, we will often come across a literary pattern called a chiasm. This is where the writer intersects mirror images of words, concepts, or events in order to draw the reader's attention to a key event, central point, or something else that the writer wants to emphasize. To help readers see the pattern, biblical scholars typically use pairs of letters (such as A with A^1 and B with B^1) to identify parallel words, phrases, or concepts when outlining a chiasm. Let's take a look at the key events of Genesis 38 by outlining them in chiastic structure.

Using the keywords, complete the outline by filling in the blanks. I completed the first one for you.

conceals   deceives   wicked   two sons   fulfilled   pledge   death

A   Judah has three sons by his unnamed <u>Canaanite</u> wife
   B   Two sons declared _____
      Levirate law is violated
      Lord puts sons to _____
      C   Judah deceives Tamar and withholds his son
         halting the continuation of the family line
         Tamar _____ her identity
           [Judah's wife dies]
         D   Judah gives Tamar his seal and staff as a _____ in exchange for sex
      C¹   Tamar _____ Judah and conceives by him
         protecting the continuation of the family line
         Tamar reveals her identity
   B¹   Tamar declared righteous
      Levirate law is _____
      Tamar spared from death
A¹   Judah has _____ by Tamar, his Canaanite daughter-in-law

Consider the center of the above chiasm. What is the significance of Judah giving Tamar his seal and staff as a pledge? What do these items represent? (Hint: glance back at page 159.)

Figuratively speaking, by handing over his seal and staff, what did Judah surrender, and what did Tamar gain?

Given that Genesis 38 is sandwiched between the beginning and end of the story of Joseph (Gen. 37, 39–50), through which we see Judah's character transformed, much of the commentary written on Genesis 38 naturally centers on Judah. However, our focus is on Tamar. After all, she experienced a remarkable transformation as well—a transformation in identity.

Praising God's Faithfulness

I have listed four phases of Tamar's story. Next to each one, briefly describe the events Tamar was experiencing.

Lost identity (verses 6-11, 19):

Hidden identity (verses 12-18):

Mistaken identity (verses 24-25):

New identity (verses 26-30):

PAUSE TO PONDER

Try to imagine yourself in Tamar's sandals. Which season of Tamar's life stirs your heart the most? Why? Now imagine if you could ask Tamar if she would have traded her place in God's story in order to be spared the trials and suffering she endured. What do you suppose she might say? Explain.

I love that God chose to weave Tamar into His grand redemptive story. One commentary author writes, "even though she was a Canaanite... She had become a heroine of the faith—despite her origins and the nature of her actions."[9]

Would you describe Tamar as a heroine? Why or why not?

Scholars are divided on their opinions of Tamar. While many commend her, there are some who condemn her. Perhaps that is not so surprising since her motivations are not clearly stated. Further, it can be challenging to understand her choices through our cultural lens. And yet, if we had to identify one person in the story who seems to exhibit at least some level of faith, it would be Tamar.

A Budding Faith

Despite her lack of conception with Er, Tamar had faith that she would conceive with Judah. Despite Judah's history of lies and betrayal, Tamar had faith that, in the end, Judah would do the right thing. On faith, Tamar surrendered Judah's seal and staff at the peril of her own life and the precious lives within her womb. As a result of Tamar's faith (along with Judah's repentance and God's great mercy), her twin sons were born.

Yet even here, it would not be easy. Like the birth of Jacob and Esau two generations before, it was as if the twins were jockeying for position. In that culture, identifying the firstborn was of utmost importance.[10] As for Tamar's sons, based on the order in which the sons of Judah are later listed in the Bible, Perez was recognized as Tamar's firstborn (see Num. 26:19–20). Here's why this is so important:

> Recall the purpose of levirate marriage by filling in the blanks with the keywords. (Hint: glance back at page 113.)
>
> widow   firstborn   relative   inherit   son
>
> It was the duty of the nearest male _____ of a deceased man to marry the childless _____ and to father her children. Her _____ son would then be acknowledged as the _____ of her deceased husband and would _____ his property.
>
> What would this mean for Tamar's son, Perez?
>
> How about Tamar? What impact would these events have on Tamar's future?

Under the levirate custom, Perez would have been considered Er's firstborn. This means that Perez would be the one to inherit the leadership role and double portion due Judah's firstborn son who died without an heir. At the same time,

Tamar would hold an honored place in Judah's family. While Judah "did not know her again" (v. 26), as the mother of Perez, Tamar's future would be secure.

On the chart on page 247, cross out the name of Judah's firstborn, Er, and write the name Perez above "Judah."

Tamar, in spite of her background and choices, is the first of only five women personally listed in the lineage of Christ. The fact that four of these women were born outside of God's covenant nation is a testimony of God's grace! The road that Tamar traveled was not easy, but in the end, God honored her faith.

.................................YOUR TURN.................................

Like Tamar, each of us will go through different seasons in life. For each description below that reflects a season in your past (not all may apply), briefly describe the circumstances. In the last column, describe how God has redeemed those circumstances, such as a lesson learned, a deepened faith, or a healed relationship.

Seasons	Describe the circumstances.	Describe how God redeemed it.
Lost identity		
Hidden identity		
Mistaken identity		
New identity		

If there is a difficult season in which you do not see God's redemption, take some time in prayer over the next few days, and ask God to reveal how He has redeemed (or is redeeming) these circumstances for your greatest good and His glory. Come back and record in the table what He reveals.

Day Five / Week Five

Next, in the same table, circle the one season that best matches how you are feeling at this time in your life.

Reflect on the season you are in right now. Take a few moments in prayer to share your heart with God. Write a prayer of praise as you feel led, acknowledging that, in Him, you are never alone, unseen, or unloved.

Lesson Summary

What Scripture, statement, or thought was most significant to you this week?*
Write it down, and reword it into a prayer of response to God.

*Share your favorite takeaway with a friend or on social media using #TamarBibleStudy. A worship song that beautifully reflects the generational blessings of knowing God is "The Blessing," by Kari Jobe.

Notes

[1] Julia Jones, *Face2Face with Tamar, Bathsheba, and Tamar: Encountering Three Women with Messed-Up Lives*, ed. Simon J. Robinson (Leominster, UK): Day One Publications, 2008), 29.

[2] *NET Bible First Edition Notes* (Richardson, TX: Biblical Studies Press, 2006), Gen. 38:26.

[3] Gordon J. Wenham, "Genesis," in *Eerdmans Commentary on the Bible*, ed. James D. G. Dunn and John W. Rogerson (Grand Rapids: William B. Eerdmans, 2003), 65.

[4] While Judah would receive the leadership position (Gen. 49:10) typically held by the firstborn son and was placed in the lineage of Christ (Matt. 1:3), it was Joseph who later received the earthly inheritance of the "double portion" that would normally go to the firstborn son (see 1 Chron. 5:1–2).

[5] Tamara Cohn Eskenazi and Tikva Frymer-Kensky, *The JPS Bible Commentary: Ruth*, First Edition (Philadelphia: Jewish Publication Society, 2011), 85.

[6] For an in-depth exploration into God's love and care for Ishmael, I encourage you to explore my Bible study *Hagar*.

[7] Martin H. Manser, *Dictionary of Bible Themes: The Accessible and Comprehensive Tool for Topical Studies* (London: Martin Manser, 2009).

[8] Steven P. Carpenter, *The Story of Joseph and Judah: A Teacher's Narrative and Structural Commentary on Genesis 37–50* (Fort Lauderdale, FL: St. Andrews House), 26.

[9] Earl D. Radmacher, Ronald Barclay Allen, and H. Wayne House, *The Nelson Study Bible: New King James Version* (Nashville: Thomas Nelson, 1997), Gen. 38:30.

[10] God would later institute regulations whereby the firstborn male of every family belonged to the Lord and therefore should be redeemed by giving a payment to the Temple treasury. (See Exod. 13:13 and Num. 18:15–16.)

NOTES

NOTES

PART III
ADOPTED

NOTES

ADOPTED INTO
FAMILY

WEEK SIX

WE HAVE CERTAINLY COVERED A LOT OF GROUND THESE past weeks! From God's promise in the garden to God's wrath in the flood to God's covenant with Abraham to God's conviction in Judah. Through it all, God is working out His plan of redemption, a plan that included Tamar and that includes you.

This week, we will witness a prophetic blessing that reverberates throughout eternity as we marvel at the glorious truth that our "names are written in heaven" (Luke 10:20).

DAY ONE
Grafted into God's Covenant Family

"Now Joseph had been brought down to Egypt . . ." These are the first words of Genesis 39. When we reach the end of Genesis 38 and read the first words of Genesis 39, it would seem that Tamar's story has come to an end, but nothing could be further from the truth. The story of Tamar is deeply intertwined in the larger story of God working in the lives of His people—and He is not finished.

For years, Genesis 38 had been considered an interruption of the Joseph story. After all, Genesis 37 ends with Judah and his brothers selling their brother Joseph into slavery. Then, the writer picks up the story of Joseph in Genesis 39 precisely where Genesis 37 left off. But nothing in Scripture is random. The story in Genesis 38 is sandwiched in between those chapters for a reason. The events occur concurrently with the events beginning in Genesis 39. When we take a closer look at the story of Tamar and Judah within the larger Genesis narrative, its importance becomes clearer. Even though Tamar's name does not appear again in the book of Genesis, Scripture is far from silent.

> Read Genesis 41:25, 28-30, 46-49, 53-54, and 42:1-4. Since Jacob had twelve sons total, Judah would have been among the ten brothers who went to Egypt. What must have transpired since we last read of Judah in Genesis 38?

During the time that Judah lived in Adullam, Joseph was slowly rising to power in Egypt. Scripture teaches that when Joseph was thirty-seven years old, "seven years of famine began . . . in all lands" (Gen. 41:54). Based on the chronology, this means that the famine began about the same year that Tamar gave birth to her twin sons. Since Judah was with his brothers when their father urged them to buy food in Egypt, it would appear that Judah had moved back to Hebron, where his father was still living. What a wonderful turn of events! Soon after Judah restores Tamar to his household and she gives birth, Judah takes another step in the right direction by reuniting with his father and brothers.

However, the famine was not over; it had only just begun. Roughly a year after Judah and his brothers return from Egypt, Jacob would ask his sons to go a second time, but there is a problem.¹ When the brothers went to Egypt the first time, Joseph (who had kept his identity hidden) placed their brother Simeon in prison, demanding that they bring back their youngest brother Benjamin. When Jacob asks his sons to return to Egypt to buy food, Judah reminds his father that Egypt's ruling official (they did not know it was Joseph) required Benjamin to accompany them.

> Read Genesis 43:8-9. What does Judah promise in response to his father's fear of letting Benjamin go to Egypt?

> Skip ahead to Genesis 44 and read verses 14, 18, and 32-34. Did Judah make good on his promise? Explain.

"The steps of a man are established by the LORD, when he delights in his way." —Psalm 37:23

Compare and contrast these events with Judah's treatment of Joseph twenty years earlier in Genesis 37:18–20 and 26–28, and answer the questions.

How had Judah changed?

Do you suppose Tamar's actions and presence in Judah's life may have played a role in these changes? Explain.

What difference do you think it might have made in Judah's life if Tamar had not asserted her levirate rights but remained a widow at her father's house?

Consider all that has transpired up to this point in the story. In what way(s) do you see God working *behind the seen* in the life of:

Judah?

Tamar?

PAUSE TO PONDER

Consider the various wrong turns and U-turns you have experienced in your own past. Where in your life has God used someone else to steer you back onto the right path? Where were you headed? What did the person do? What difference do you think it might have made if the person had not crossed your path? Looking back, do you see God at work *behind the seen* in your life? Explain.

Adopted into God's Family

Interesting fact: God often led His people into Egypt during famines in order to prevent their assimilation with foreign nations. The threat of assimilation did not exist in Egypt, because Egyptians did not intermarry with foreigners.[2]

A Costly Pledge

In the book of Genesis, the word translated *pledge* appears in the context of only two events: when Judah surrenders his staff and seal to Tamar and when Judah offers himself in place of his youngest brother Benjamin. While this is a wonderful picture of Judah's changed heart, the greater picture is what God is doing *behind the seen*. Let's see what happens next in this complex family drama.

Read Genesis 45:1-11 and 25-28. Briefly summarize the events.

Read Genesis 46:29-30 and 47:11-12. Briefly summarize the events.

The family of Jacob is reunited at last. The brothers have reconciled, Jacob embraces the son he believed had died, and Jacob's family settles in the land of Egypt. Interestingly, it is the story of Judah and Tamar that helps to illuminate the story of Joseph and his brothers. To see it clearly, we will look at several events from both stories, noting key contrasts in one last chiastic structure.

Complete the outline by filling in the blanks using the keywords. I completed the first one for you.

himself   reveals   reconcile   two sons   moves   famine

A   Judah and his brothers *betray* Joseph who is enslaved in Egypt
   B   Judah moves away from his father and brothers
      Judah starts a family, but God strikes his _____ dead
      C   _____ strikes the land
         Brothers go to Egypt for food
         D   Joseph conceals his identity from his brothers
            E   Judah offers _____ as a pledge in exchange for his brother Benjamin's freedom
         D¹   Joseph _____ his identity to his brothers
      C¹   Famine continues in the land
         Joseph provides his brothers with food in Egypt
   B¹   Judah _____ into the land with his father and brothers
      Judah's two new sons continue the family line (Gen. 46:12)
A¹   Judah and his brothers _____ with Joseph in Egypt

Glance back at the chiasm you completed earlier on page 201. Complete the table by comparing the significance of the pledge as reflected in the two chiasms. I completed one for you.

	Story of Judah and Tamar	**Story of Joseph and His Brothers**
Who gave the pledge?	*Judah*	
What pledge was given?		
Why was it given? What was it exchanged for?		

Consider the table and Judah's choices. What conclusions can you draw?

How does the change in Judah's character, as revealed through these events, help shed light on the significance of Tamar's role in his life and family?

At this point in the story, roughly twenty-two years have passed since Joseph was sold into slavery and Judah moved away from his family and settled in Adullam. This means that Judah and Tamar's twin sons were still infants when the family settled in Egypt.[3]

Pause here for a moment, and try to imagine what this move might have been like for Tamar. Apart from physical possessions:

List two or three things Tamar would have left behind.

List two or three things Tamar would have gained.

Describe two or three challenges Tamar may have faced.

Adopted into God's Family

Considering the three lists you made, which aspect of Tamar's experiences tugs on your heart the most? Why?

Which aspect of her changed life can you relate to personally? Explain.

From Foreigner to Family

Optional: read Genesis 46:8–27.

God never does anything halfway. After the birth of their sons, God could have left Tamar and Judah to themselves, but He was not finished. Even though Judah had reunited with his father and brothers in Hebron, the family was still fractured. And nothing short of a widespread famine would bring them back together.

After recounting the details of Jacob and his sons settling in Egypt, the writer goes on to list Jacob's grandsons in Genesis 46:8–27. At first, we may be tempted to gloss over the list of names, but remember, nothing in Scripture is random. Notice that none of Jacob's great-grandsons are mentioned except the names of the sons born to Judah and Tamar's son, Perez. One commentary author explains, "Judah sired five clans in all. Since two died out in Canaan, two of the second generation are listed to complete the five to be credited to Judah. Only Perez's sons are named because his was the most important of the clans: David was his descendant."[4] In short, even though Judah and Tamar's sons were infants when they entered Egypt, the future sons of Perez are mentioned, foreshadowing their significance in the genealogy and in God's redemptive story.

Nevertheless, there is nothing in Scripture to suggest that life suddenly became easy for Tamar after her sons were born. What happened after Judah brought her "home" to Hebron? Did Jacob embrace Tamar as a daughter? Did Judah's brothers' wives embrace Tamar as a sister? While we are not told how Judah's family viewed her, we do know how Tamar was perceived by later generations.

In addition to listing the descendants of Perez, there is another distinguishing feature in the genealogy of Genesis 46. While the writer makes it a point to identify one grandson as "the son of a Canaanite woman" (Simeon's son Shaul), as well as Joseph's sons born to his Egyptian wife, "Asenath, the daughter of Potiphera the priest of On" (Gen. 46:10, 20), he never mentions Tamar's nationality.

Sometimes when Scripture is silent, it speaks louder than words. While the writer made it a point to reference grandsons born to foreign women, it would seem that he felt it unnecessary to include Tamar in a similar category. Taken together with additional passages that we will explore tomorrow, this suggests that by the time Genesis was written, Tamar was not viewed as a foreigner but as a member of God's covenant family.

............................YOUR TURN............................

Let not the foreigner who has joined himself to the LORD say, "The LORD will surely separate me from his people."

Isaiah 56:3a

I love God's heart for the outcast and for those who are most vulnerable. When we consider all that had transpired in young Tamar's life in such a short time, what would appear to some as a marvelous reversal of fortune is nothing less than God's divine intervention. One minute we see a young foreign widow condemned to death, and the next we see her grafted into God's family.

> Consider Isaiah 56:3a, printed above, along with Psalm 146:9 in the margin. Despite all that Tamar had against her, what do these verses reveal about God's character?

"The LORD watches over the sojourners; he upholds the widow and the fatherless." —Psalm 146:9

How about you? Is there something you believe (or have believed) hinders you from:

- being a part of God's family? Explain.

- fulfilling the work of the ministry He has called you to? Explain.

- becoming all that God desires you to be? Explain.

Adopted into God's Family

Spend some time with the Lord; ask Him to reveal any steps of faith you need to take. Write a prayer of commitment as He leads you.

DAY TWO
Anticipating the Coming King

When I became a Christian more than twenty years ago, I initially focused my Bible reading on the New Testament. I especially enjoyed the gospels as I loved learning all about Jesus's life and ministry. However, when I began reading the Old Testament, God opened my eyes to His Word in ways I never could have imagined. I was awestruck by the beauty of how everything in the Bible ties together. To this day, the more time I spend in God's Word, the more I fall in love with Jesus, since it all points to Him.

PAUSE TO PONDER

> What is your favorite book from the Old Testament and why? How about the New Testament? What is your favorite book and why?

Through the years, there is one biblical story I have read again and again; for as long as I have been a Christian, it has been one of my favorite Bible stories. It's the book of Ruth. If the story of Judah and Tamar is a picture of levirate marriage gone wrong, the story of Ruth and Boaz is a picture of levirate marriage gone right. While we can only do a condensed overview, it will be worth it, I promise. However, before we dive into Ruth, we first need to wrap up the final chapters concerning Jacob and his sons, as these will provide critical context as we move forward.

A Prophetic Blessing

Read Genesis 48:1-4, 21; 49:1, 28, and 33. Briefly summarize the events by filling in the blanks with the keywords.

prophecy   land   sons   blessing

When Joseph learns that his father is ill, he brings to him his two _____. Jacob recounts God's _____ on his family and assures Joseph that God will be with him and will bring him back to the _____ God promised them. Israel then speaks a _____ (or a blessing) over each of his sons before he dies.

After the elderly Jacob (whom God renamed "Israel") was reunited with his beloved son Joseph, he settled in the land of Goshen in Egypt with his family. When Jacob knew his time of death was drawing near, he gathered his twelve sons together and spoke of their descendants' future.

Read Genesis 49:8-10, which is a portion of the prophetic blessing spoken by Jacob over his son, Judah. Then answer the questions that follow.

How does Judah live up to the name his mother, Leah, gave him, according to the first part of Genesis 49:8?

Symbolically, what does a scepter or staff represent? Circle all that apply. (Hint: glance back at the "Stolen Identity" section of Day Four of Week Four.)

authority   birthright   royalty   social status

Compare and contrast the last part of Genesis 49:8 with Genesis 37:5-7 and 42:6-8. Which son is ultimately made leader over the others?

How do you suppose the news of Judah's leadership and royal line would have affected Tamar, whose sons are now around nineteen years old based on Genesis 47:28?

Interesting fact: after the Babylonian captivity, those who returned to the Promised Land were mostly from the tribe of Judah. As such, the land came to be called Judea and the people, Jews.

Adopted into God's Family

When studying the Bible, reading different English translations can be beneficial. For example, the literal translation of the second half of Genesis 49:10 can be challenging to understand in some versions. The New International Version offers a helpful translation: "The scepter will not depart from Judah, nor the ruler's staff from between his feet, until he to whom it belongs shall come and the obedience of the nations shall be his."

In other words, God is revealing that the descendants of Judah will hold the scepter and staff (symbols of royalty and authority) until the Messiah comes. That is, a line of kings will come from Judah, ultimately leading to the One to whom all authority and kingship belongs. This blessing over Judah is the first biblical prophecy to specifically reference a messianic king.[5]

The Patient Plan of God

As significant as the prophecy spoken over Judah was, God waited ten generations before anointing the first king descended from Judah. God seems to prefer working out His plan in stages. Along the way, we see the beauty of His redemptive plan slowly unfolding. Just as God used Judah's detours to graft foreign-born Tamar into His covenant family, He used another family's detour to graft yet another foreign-born woman into the genealogy. The events take place precisely seven generations after Judah.

> What is the significance of the number seven in the Bible? Fill in one or both of the blanks based on what we learned in our first day of study. (Hint: glance back at the end of the lesson in Day One of Week One.)
>
> In the Bible, the number seven is symbolic for _____ or _____.

At the start of today's lesson, I proposed that if the story of Judah and Tamar is a picture of levirate marriage gone wrong, the story of Ruth and Boaz is a picture of levirate marriage gone right. How fitting that Boaz appears precisely seven generations after Judah, providing God's people with a tender picture of what levirate marriage should look like and also what it means to be a kinsman-redeemer.

> Pause here for a moment and consider what we have learned about Boaz's mother, Rahab. Check all that apply. (Hint: glance back at Joshua 2:1–21.)
>
> Rahab was:
>
> ☐ a foreigner
>
> ☐ a God-fearer
>
> ☐ a prostitute

"He rejected the tent of Joseph; he did not choose the tribe of Ephraim, but he chose the tribe of Judah, Mount Zion, which he loves."
—Psalm 78:67-68

Rahab's background and the fact that she risked her life to escape the trap of prostitution and seek refuge in God would have played a significant role in Boaz's view of foreigners, prostitutes, and women in general. It is no coincidence that God would choose Boaz, whose mother was both a foreigner and a prostitute, to protect and redeem Ruth, as we will soon discover.

In order to see how God weaves the story of Boaz and Ruth together with the story of Judah and Tamar, we will finish today's lesson by looking at several highlights from Ruth 1–3. Tomorrow, we will explore the final segment of Ruth, which culminates with a blessing that highlights the remarkable place Tamar has in God's unfolding plan.

Note: the readings for Ruth 1 and Ruth 2 are optional; the exercises can be completed with or without reading the passages.

 Optional: read Ruth 1:1–18.

In the left column are key events taken from Ruth 1:1–18. For each event, underline one or two keywords or phrases that are similar to the events we read in Genesis 38. Then, in the right column, briefly describe the corresponding events from Genesis 38 (you may notice parallels, contrasts, or both). I included Scripture references if you need them. I completed the first and last ones for you.

Story of Ruth and Boaz	Story of Tamar and Judah
A man, along with his wife Naomi and two sons, went away from their homeland to wait out a famine in Moab.	Judah left his homeland and family and moved to a foreign land where he married and had three sons (Gen. 38:1–5).
While there, Naomi's husband died, and she became a widow.	(Gen. 38:12)
Her two sons married Moabite women, but both sons died ten years later.	(Gen. 38:6–10)
Naomi tried to set her daughters-in-law free by urging them to return home to their families and seek new husbands, saying, "would you therefore wait till [I remarried, had more sons, and] they were grown?"	(Gen. 38:11)
but Ruth refused to abandon her mother-in-law, saying, "Your people shall be my people, and your God my God."	but Tamar refused to abandon her place within her father-in-law's family (Gen. 38:13–18, 24–26).

Adopted into God's Family

Ponder the table; which pair of events from the two stories stands out to you the most? Why?

Optional: read Ruth 1:22 and 2:1-3, 8-12, and 19-20.

In the Bible, a redeemer (or kinsman-redeemer) is someone who pays a price on behalf of an impoverished relative to release the relative from slavery or the relative's property from mortgage.[6]

Ruth 1 ends with Naomi and Ruth leaving Moab and arriving in Bethlehem at the beginning of the barley harvest. Like Tamar, Ruth is a young, foreign, childless widow. Being in poverty, Ruth finds herself gleaning in a field of a wealthy landowner named Boaz. When Boaz notices her and inquires who she is, he realizes she is the faithful Moabite daughter-in-law of Naomi, of whom he had heard a good report.

Instead of taking advantage of Ruth's poverty and vulnerability, Boaz provides for her, even instructing his men not to harm her. When Ruth returns to her mother-in-law and tells her all that happened, Naomi is encouraged to realize that the man who took notice and care of Ruth was a close relative, a redeemer (Ruth 2:20).

For the following exercises, please read Ruth 3:1-17 in your Bible. Listed below are several facts and events taken from the stories of Tamar and Ruth. Next to each one, circle either True or False. I completed the first row for you.

Story of Tamar (Gen. 38:12-20)		Story of Ruth (Ruth 3:1-17)	
Tamar is a young foreign childless widow and daughter-in-law to a member of God's covenant family.	**True** / False	Ruth is a young, foreign, childless widow and daughter-in-law to a member of God's covenant family.	**True** / False
A celebration is at hand.	True / False	A celebration is at hand.	True / False
Tamar is told where Judah will be.	True / False	Ruth is told where Boaz will be.	True / False
Tamar is hidden under a garment.	True / False	Ruth is hidden under a garment.	True / False

Day Two / Week Six

Judah asks Tamar to identify herself.	True False	Boaz asks Ruth to identify herself.	True False
Judah assumes Tamar is a prostitute.	True False	Boaz fears Ruth could be mistaken for a prostitute.	True False
Tamar solicits Judah.	True False	Ruth solicits Boaz.	True False
Judah protects Tamar's honor by not touching her.	True False	Boaz protects Ruth's honor by not touching her.	True False
Tamar disappears before anyone can identify her.	True False	Ruth disappears before anyone can identify her.	True False
Judah sends Tamar away with only a pledge for payment.	True False	Boaz sends Ruth away with a generous gift of food.	True False

Compare and contrast Judah's actions with Boaz's. Despite the fact that Judah did not know it was Tamar whom he met, how does Boaz's treatment of Ruth reflect God's heart toward women?

In Ruth 3:14, Boaz says, "Let it not be known that the woman came to the threshing floor." This warning is no small matter and is one of the key contrasts between the two stories. The threshing floor, as well as the location of the sheep shearing in the story of Judah, were places where men could expect to find prostitutes. The men were far from home, drinking and celebration was taking place, and immoral behavior could easily be kept secret. Therefore, if it were discovered that Ruth visited the threshing floor, both Ruth and Boaz's reputations would be in danger. In the minds of the people in Bethlehem, there could only be one kind of woman who would be lurking around the threshing floor at night—a prostitute.

But Ruth willingly obeys Naomi's explicit instructions. Boldly lying at Boaz's feet, Ruth silently communicates her desperate situation while simultaneously trusting in Naomi's wisdom and Boaz's noble character. What courage! And what a contrast. Whereas Judah was willing to solicit a prostitute in broad daylight, Boaz, even under the cover of darkness, is careful to protect not only his own conscience before God, but also his and Ruth's reputations.

The glaring dichotomy between these stories is one of the reasons why I love studying God's Word. When I look back on my life, I can relate far more to Judah and Tamar than I can to Ruth and Boaz. Yet both stories fill me with hope. Judah, Tamar, Boaz, and Ruth—each of them reminds me of what God can do in the lives of those who seek Him. While it's hard to miss the beauty of redemption in the book of Ruth, for many of us, our real-life experiences may seem more in line with those of Judah and Tamar. Wrong turns. Detours. Vying for control. Deceiving and being deceived. But I love the fact that God never abandoned them there, and because He is faithful, He never abandons us.

....YOUR TURN..

Describe one way that you have been blessed by studying God's Word these past weeks.

What part of our study of Tamar in particular is most memorable to you?

Spend some time in prayer, asking God to reveal one or two people among your family and friends who might be blessed by doing this study. Reach out to them, and share one thing you have learned. Come back and record their response(s) and any other steps God asks you to take.

DAY THREE
Seeing God's Redemption Unfold

Before I became a Christian, *Pretty Woman* was one of my favorite movies. It had glamour, action, drama, and a girl's tried-and-true favorite: rescue by a knight in shining armor. Only after God opened my eyes to His pure and holy love was I able to recognize the sinister flaw in the movie: the "hero" who rescued the prostitute was also her customer. It's a perfect picture of distorted love, redemption, and salvation.

Maybe that's why now, as a Christian, I'm so attracted to the story of Boaz and Ruth, especially in light of the generations that lived before them. When we trace the generations beginning with God's covenant with Abraham, we witness many struggles and failures along the way, particularly in regard to marriage and sexuality:

- Abraham and Sarah using Hagar rather than trusting in God's timing (Gen. 16:1–4)
- Isaac's willingness to put his wife at risk in order to protect himself (Gen. 26:6–7)
- Jacob getting entangled in polygamy (Gen. 29)
- Judah's reckless use of a prostitute (Gen. 38:15–18)

In one sense, we can be grateful that these stories are included in the Bible. They remind us of God's mercy—the beautiful aspect of God's character that compels Him to respond with love and compassion toward the broken and hurting, whether they are broken by sin or circumstance. The stories also remind us of God's grace as we see Him working through the stumbling steps of His people instead of abandoning them in their sin. When I look back on the failures of my own past—sexual depravity, abortion, divorce—I cannot help but fall to my knees in worship, praising God for His forgiveness and mercy!

PAUSE TO PONDER

> Name one way God has shown you mercy this past week. Why is His mercy so important? What difference does it make? Is there someone to whom God is asking you to show mercy? What recent act of mercy have you experienced that you can give God praise for today?

Seven generations after Judah and Tamar, we are introduced to Boaz. Here is a man who not only fulfills the duty of levirate marriage as written in the law (Deut. 25:5) but fulfills the spirit of the law in his heart. Boaz's selfless choices and tender mercy toward a vulnerable young foreign widow (the daughter-in-law of his relative Naomi, who risked being taken for a prostitute) serve to symbolically right the wrongs of his ancestor Judah's treatment of his own daughter-in-law, likewise a young foreign widow desperate enough to pose as a prostitute seven

> God's character compels Him to respond with love and compassion toward the broken and hurting, whether they are broken by sin or circumstance.

generations earlier. In short, the story of Boaz and Ruth is a glimpse of the redemption that is coming.

We pick up the story just after Ruth leaves Boaz at the threshing floor, where she had come in the middle of the night and proposed marriage—a bold move for a woman in that day.

Read Ruth 4:1-2. Briefly describe the events.

Boaz held a high standing in the community. He not only sat at the town gate (the place where elders would sit and judge disputes and decide other important matters), but he also had no difficulty quickly summoning ten elders to hear what he had to say. In effect, Boaz would have been considered a ruler, or patriarch, in the community.

Read Ruth 4:3-6; compare and contrast the events with Genesis 38:8-9. List one or two similarities and one or two differences between the two sets of events.

Similarities:

Differences:

What was each man willing to take?

The nearer redeemer (not Boaz):

Onan:

What was each man unwilling to give up?

The nearer redeemer (not Boaz):

Day Three / Week Six

Onan:

 Compare Ruth 4:5-6 with Genesis 38:14. What same right was being neglected for both women?

Taking a Risk

Underneath all the similarities between the two stories are two women suffering the same violation of justice: each one was denied her rights under levirate practice. In Ruth, the unnamed relative was eager to take over Naomi's property but was unwilling to care for a vulnerable widow or provide a son to carry on the name of his deceased relative.

In the end, both Tamar and Ruth boldly laid claim to their rights. Admittedly, Tamar's solution was far less graceful than Ruth's (perhaps not so surprising when we consider that Ruth, unlike Tamar, lived under the caring guidance of her Israelite mother-in-law for more than ten years [Ruth 1:4]). Nevertheless, even Judah ultimately looked past Tamar's methods and instead acknowledged the injustice Tamar suffered, declaring, "She is more righteous than I."

Considering both accounts, one commentator writes, "Ruth, like Tamar, takes risks; she provokes a patriarch . . . to do the right thing."[7]

What was Boaz willing to sacrifice (or risk) in order to provide for both Ruth and Naomi's security? Place a checkmark next to each one that applies.

- ☐ Reputation (for marrying a foreigner)
- ☐ Cost to buy back Naomi's property
- ☐ Ruth might be barren (though married for ten years, she was still childless)
- ☐ Firstborn son (who would legally become the son and heir of Mahlon)
- ☐ Expense of providing for Naomi (and Ruth)
- ☐ His own son as his legal heir (if Ruth only births one son)

Which sacrifice do you suppose was most difficult? Why? (Note: This question is designed for discussion purposes. As the response calls for speculation, there are no right or wrong answers.)

Finding Comfort in God's Word

After my divorce, God blessed me with a loving couple who welcomed me into their family and home. During those early years in my Christian walk, several scriptures became especially meaningful to me. One of these was the simple verse of Psalm 68:6. Another was the book of Ruth, which stirred my heart for its tender portrayal of what seemed to me the picture-perfect husband. But even more than those was a passage from Isaiah 54. While the passage was written in the context of God's commitment to His beloved nation Israel, the general principles also apply to all who belong to Him. When I ponder the life of Tamar and all she endured, I cannot help but wonder what she might have felt had Isaiah's words been spoken over her, just as God had used them to speak over me.

> Read Isaiah 54:4-8 below. Underline every name and title (formal and informal) God uses of Himself. Next, place a circle around every promise He makes.

Fear not, for you will not be ashamed;
be not confounded, for you will not be disgraced;
for you will forget the shame of your youth,
and the reproach of your widowhood you will remember no more.
For your Maker is your husband,
the Lord of hosts is his name;
and the Holy One of Israel is your Redeemer,
the God of the whole earth he is called.
For the Lord has called you
like a wife deserted and grieved in spirit,
like a wife of youth when she is cast off,
says your God.
For a brief moment I deserted you,
but with great compassion I will gather you.
In overflowing anger for a moment
I hid my face from you,
but with everlasting love I will have compassion on you,"
says the Lord, your Redeemer.

"God sets the lonely in families." —Psalm 68:6 NIV

PAUSE TO PONDER

> Reflecting on the names and titles you underlined in Isaiah 54:4-8, which aspect of God:
>
> Are you most grateful for right now? Why?
>
> Do you need in your life most right now? Why?
>
> Of the promises you circled in the passage, which one:
>
> Are you most grateful for right now? Why?
>
> Do you need in your life most right now? Why?

An Unexpected Blessing

While my heart is drawn to the "love story" embodied in the book of Ruth, after spending a year studying Tamar's story, God opened my eyes to a passage in Ruth that I had previously given little thought to. In Ruth 4, after the nearer kinsman rejects his role as redeemer, Boaz purchases the land and Ruth as his wife, after which the people speak an intriguing blessing. Let's take a look.

> Read Ruth 4:11-12. Although Ruth had been married to Mahlon ten years during which she bore no children, what blessing of assurance do the people speak over Boaz:
>
> Concerning Ruth (verse 11)?
>
>
>
> Concerning his offspring (verse 12)?

The blessing over Ruth to be like Rachel and Leah is a precious reminder that, despite all that the sisters endured, God had made a covenant with Jacob, and both Rachel and Leah are honored for their role in building up the house of Israel, a people set apart by God for His good purposes. But the blessing continues.

> Of all the women and families in God's covenant nation who lived in prior generations, why do you suppose the blessing spoken to Boaz was also tied to

the son birthed through Tamar's union with Judah? In the margin, list as many reasons as you can think of. (Hint: consider the various parallels between the stories of Ruth and Boaz and Judah and Tamar.)

The people and elders could have chosen any number of women or families as a model for their blessing. How encouraging that they chose to include Tamar! Rather than focusing on the sordid details, they saw hope! Tamar's hope for a child, her courage to right the wrong done to her, and her desire to be included in God's family could not be a more fitting blessing on Ruth and Boaz.

The blessing may also serve to acknowledge the fact that both women were foreigners. Not only were God's people forbidden to marry Canaanites (Deut. 7:1–4), but Deuteronomy 23:3 commands, "No . . . Moabite may . . . enter the assembly of the Lord forever." And yet, God was pleased to welcome Tamar (a Canaanite), Ruth (a Moabite), and even Rahab (a foreigner *and* a prostitute)! But that's not all. Being a lavish God, He does even more.

After Boaz marries Ruth, she gives birth to a son. The women of the town bless not only the child, but Ruth also, declaring to Naomi, "your daughter-in-law who loves you . . . is [worth] more to you than seven sons" (Ruth 4:15). A daughter-in-law is worth more than seven sons? How can this be in a patriarchal society that placed such high value on sons? The answer is found in the last verses of the book.

Read Ruth 4:18–22, and answer the questions.

Name the first and last persons listed in the genealogy.

What reason would the writer have for starting the genealogy where he did? (Hint: glance back at Genesis 49:10.)

Just as foreign-born Ruth was recognized as a faithful daughter-in-law to Naomi, the people are reminded of another foreign daughter-in-law who likewise sought, even fought, to hold on to her place in God's family. The book of Ruth ends with a genealogy leading to the hope of the nation's beloved future king, David—a genealogy that would not exist had it not been for Tamar's resolve and God's faithfulness. Nothing in all creation could ever stand in the way of God's plan of redemption; nevertheless, by choosing to include Tamar in His story, we

Day Three / Week Six

are blessed with the precious reminder that our redemption is not dependent on our choices, whether good or bad, but on His.

> On the chart on page 247, cross out the name of Eliab, who was the firstborn of David's father Jesse (see 1 Sam. 16:1-13 and 17:13), and write the name David above "Perez."

................................YOUR TURN................................

At the beginning of today's lesson, I referred to the movie *Pretty Woman*, which I would now describe as a picture of distorted love, redemption, and salvation. In contrast, God's Word paints a glorious picture of a love so holy that not even Boaz can measure up. Instead, he serves as a pointer to the only One who can offer true love, redemption, and salvation.

> Look back at the passage printed from Isaiah 54 earlier in today's lesson, along with the Pause to Ponder questions that followed it. Spend some time with the Lord in prayer. Share the longings of your heart with Him, as well as the things you are grateful for. Write a prayer of praise and petition to the LORD, your Redeemer, who loves you with everlasting love.

> "Blessed is the one you choose and bring near, to dwell in your courts!"
> —Psalm 65:4a

DAY FOUR
Awaiting the Glory to Be Revealed

Over the past weeks, we have traced the unfolding of God's redemptive story through the generations of man, from Adam to Noah and from Abraham to David, each generation waiting for their Savior, each woman praying she would give birth to the Messiah (Gen. 3:15).

> Write Galatians 4:4 below.

On the chart on page 247, above "David," write the name Jesus.

Generations had waited for this moment in history. Then one day, the time had finally come. Jesus could have chosen anyone to be a part of His human ancestry. For reasons known only in the mind of God, He chose Tamar to bear the son who would carry on the royal line of Judah until it reached the One to whom it ultimately belongs (see Gen. 49:10). After four hundred years of silence, God finally spoke, choosing to begin the New Testament with these words:

> The book of the genealogy of Jesus Christ, the son of David, the son of Abraham. Abraham was the father of Isaac, and Isaac the father of Jacob, and Jacob the father of Judah and his brothers, and Judah the father of Perez and Zerah by Tamar. (Matt. 1:1–3)

Your Days Are Written in His Book

Can you imagine your name being etched in God's eternal Word, let alone in the lineage of Christ? During Tamar's lifetime, no one would have envied her. Many would condemn her. Perhaps one or two had pity. Hers was a life that otherwise would have disappeared in the pages of history, but God had a different plan.

> "All the days ordained for me were written in your book before one of them came to be."
> —Psalm 139:16 NIV

PAUSE TO PONDER

When did you first become aware of God's presence in your life? Since that time, what difference has it made:

to you?

to your family?

to friends and others in your social circle?

Consider what your life might look like today if God had *not* stepped in. Take a few moments to give Him thanks for His presence in your life.

Imagine if God had chosen to record your name in the lineage of Christ. What thoughts come to mind? Is this idea a struggle for you? Explain.

Day Four / Week Six

🍃 Reflect on Tamar's background and choices. What does God's willingness to invite Tamar into the lineage of the Messiah reveal about God's character? (Hint: see 1 Corinthians 1:27-29 and John 15:16a.)

Scripture teaches that in the beginning, God created human beings in His image (Gen. 1:26–27). After sin entered the world, that image became marred, but in His grace, God did not abandon us in our sin. Instead, He promised that through Eve's offspring, a Savior would one day come (Gen. 3:15). Toward that end, God has been actively working through the generations of man, setting apart a people to call His own, a people to reflect His love and proclaim His name in a lost and broken world.

Galatians 4:4 is printed below. Finish the sentence by writing verse 5.

But when the fullness of time had come, God sent forth his Son, born of woman, born under the law, _____

_____.

Adopted into God's Family

God's Word tells us that all who trust in Christ are "born again" (John 3:3–7) and become "children of God" (John 1:12–13). These concepts are rich and profound all by themselves, but God is a lavish, loving Father. He doesn't stop there.

Why do you suppose that, in addition to being born again as a child of God, believers are also "adopted" into God's family? List as many reasons as you can think of. (Hint: What aspects of earthly adoption could be applied to spiritual adoption?)

> "But to all who did receive him, who believed in his name, he gave the right to become children of God." —John 1:12

For six years, I had the joy and privilege of serving on the board of directors for our local life-affirming pregnancy care clinics. While serving in this role, one thing I learned early on was how adoption was presented to a woman who did not plan to raise her child herself. Today, we often hear it described as "giving up your child for adoption." However, at the pregnancy care clinics, the woman was asked, "Do you want to make an adoption plan for your child?"

Compare and contrast the two descriptions of adoption by reading each one out loud and writing several positive or negative aspects that come to mind.

Give up your child.   Make an adoption plan.

Adoption is not about giving up or giving in; rather, it's about the mother (perhaps the father as well) choosing the best possible family for her child. No matter the circumstances that lead up to it, at the end of the day, adoption is a decision born out of love and sacrifice.

Read Ephesians 1:3-6 in your Bible. Fill in the missing words below based on the passage.

Blessed be the God and Father of our Lord Jesus Christ, who has blessed us in Christ with _____ spiritual blessing in the heavenly places, even as he _____ us in him _____ the foundation of the world, that we should be holy and blameless before him. In love he predestined us for _____ to himself as sons through Jesus Christ, according to the purpose of his will, to the praise of his glorious grace, with which he has blessed us in the Beloved.

In the left column, rewrite each fill-in word from the previous exercise in the order that they appear in the original passage. In the right column, share what each truth means to you personally.

Complete the fill-in word based on the previous exercise.	What does this mean to you personally?
You are blessed in Christ with _____ spiritual blessing in the heavenly places.	
He _____ you [to be holy and blameless before Him; that is, to be conformed to the image of His son].	

Day Four / Week Six

He made His decision concerning you _____ the foundation of the world.	
In love, God the Father made an _____ plan for you to belong to Him forever.	

These are precious truths!

Before the foundation of the world, our heavenly Father made an adoption plan for each one of us—a plan to give us a new name, an eternal home, and a heritage forever. God knew from eternity past every mistake and failure we would make, and yet our past mistakes can never exclude us; our future failures will never disqualify us. Our adoption papers were written from eternity past—signed not in ink, but in blood.

PAUSE TO PONDER

Did you know that writing something by hand will significantly improve your ability to recall the information later? Reading these wonderful truths is one thing, but taking a few moments to write them out by hand will help solidify them in your mind and heart. In the space below (or, if you prefer, on one of the blank notes pages), rewrite the previous paragraph. However, this time, make it personal by replacing the plural pronouns with personal pronouns (use *me* instead of *us*, *my* instead of *our*, *I* instead of *we*). The first sentence is printed for you.

Before the foundation of the world, my heavenly Father made an adoption plan for me.

> As believers, our adoption papers were written from eternity past—signed not in ink, but in blood.

Consider writing the above paragraph in your journal or on a note card to keep as a reminder.

Adopted into God's Family

The Privilege of Adoption

Interestingly, Old Testament Hebrew does not have a word for *adoption*. One commentary author suggests that its absence "may be explained in part by alternatives to infertile marriages. Levirate marriages lessened the need for adoption, and the principle of maintaining property within the tribe . . . allayed some of the fears of childless parents."[8]

But throughout Scripture, we see the beautiful concept of adoption, such as in the stories of Moses (Exod. 2:1–10; Acts 7:21), Esther (Esther 2:5–7), and Jacob's "adoption" of Joseph's sons (Gen. 48:1–6). In one sense, even Jesus was adopted! Nevertheless, when the apostle Paul refers to adoption as representing the spiritual status of believers, he is not envisioning adoption in terms of a child in need of parents or a home. Scripture already teaches that believers become children of God; instead, Paul has something else in mind.

In order to grasp it more fully, we need to do a brief Greek word study of the word *adoption* as it is used in the New Testament. A literal translation of its usage in Ephesians 1:5 would be "adoption as sons." Biblical scholars recognize that in the New Testament, the expression "sons of God," like the word *brothers*, represents all believers, both male and female siblings within God's family. In the same way, "adoption as sons" in Ephesians 1:5 (also in Romans 8 and Galatians 4) applies to the spiritual adoption of *all* believers (both male and female). However, in order for us to understand the ramifications of this tremendous truth, we need to examine the meaning of the text as it would have been understood by the early church to whom Paul was writing.

> In biblical times, what reason(s) might legal adoption have related specifically to sons, rather than both sons and daughters? (Hint: see Gen. 15:1–4.)

Bible study tip: before attempting to apply a passage to one's own life, it is important to know how the biblical writer intended the passage to be understood by the original audience.

The phrase translated "adoption as sons" is one word in Greek: *huiothesia*.[9] It is a legal term derived from the combination of two Greek words: *huios*, "a son," and *thesis*, "a placing." The word "signifies the place and condition of a son given to one to whom it does not naturally belong."[10] In other words, it gives a person legal standing as a son having both the privileges (i.e., inheritance rights) and duties of a son.

As mentioned earlier in today's lesson, Scripture teaches that believers become members of God's family when we are born again as children of God. Paul adds the language of adoption because adoption has to do with the legal transaction of giving the position and privileges of a son. Why a son and not a daughter? Because in Roman culture (Paul is writing to Gentile churches located within the Roman Empire), the term was used to legally designate a male heir (very often an adult) since inheritance rights were typically passed on to sons.[11] Paul's teaching on adoption is not about gender; it's about position. Both male and female believers are *huiothesia* ("adopted as sons") in the sense that they have been given a new legal standing and privileges they did not possess before.

> Read Romans 8:14-15. In what way(s) are you able to enjoy the experience of spiritual adoption right now?

> Read Romans 8:22-23. What aspect of your spiritual adoption must you wait to experience in the future?

From the day we become children of God to the day we enter glory, you and I exist simultaneously within two realms. On earth, where our physical bodies are confined by time and space, we are blessed with the indwelling of God's Holy Spirit and the security of knowing our heavenly Father watches over us. However, in the spiritual realm, we are already "raised" and "seated" with Christ (Eph. 2:6) as fellow heirs with Him (Rom. 8:17).[12] Imagine what our lives would be like if we lived every day in light of the glory that awaits all who hope in Him.

............................YOUR TURN............................

> How often, on average, do you ponder the glory of heaven that God has promised you as His beloved child? Circle one.
>
>   weekly   monthly   rarely   never
>
> *If you answered weekly or monthly:*
>
> What aspect of your heavenly home do you look forward to the most? Explain.

If you answered rarely or never:

How might your outlook on life change if you incorporated more time meditating on the hope of glory that is yours in Christ?

What one step will you take to move forward in this area?

A passage of Scripture that I have been clinging to lately is Psalm 73:23-26. Open your Bible, and spend a few moments meditating on this passage. What one truth stands out to you the most? Rewrite it below as a prayer of praise.

DAY FIVE
Your Name Is Written in Heaven

Throughout our lives, each of us will feel like we do not fit in at one time or another. As I shared earlier, I wasn't raised in the church, so when God called me to seminary, I was keenly aware of my messy past: drug and alcohol abuse, promiscuity, abortion, divorce—not to mention my lack of Christian heritage and Bible knowledge. If this was not difficult enough, I was nearly twice the age of most of my classmates. One morning during my first semester, I walked into the break room where a group of students were discussing the theological teaching of a person named Calvin. At the time, I was too embarrassed to admit that the only Calvin I knew was a guy famous for his designer jeans.

My ignorance came to light a few months later at a Christmas party hosted by one of my professors and his wife. A game, modeled after the TV game show *Name That Tune*, was arranged, whereby guests were divided into teams and each team had a sheet of paper to record the names of ten songs. After the first few notes were played, the teams had thirty seconds to collaborate for each song. Whichever team guessed the most correct songs won.

I ended up on the team with my professor, which I thought was fun, until it soon became apparent that I would be little help. Many of the tunes were church hymns or traditional Christmas songs. Not being raised in the church, I simply did not recognize them fast enough. By the fifth song, I was a little embarrassed by my inability to contribute, especially with my professor sitting right next to me. The sixth song came and went—then the seventh, the eighth, and the ninth.

Just when I thought it was over, my redemption came. When I heard the first notes of the last song, I nearly jumped from my seat, blurting out, "Grandma Got Run Over by a Reindeer!" I had the right answer, but I immediately noticed that I was the *only* one in my group to recognize the song (which apparently had been included as a joke). If I felt like I didn't fit in before, well . . .

I loved the years I spent in seminary. While they were some of the most challenging years of my life, they were also some of the most rewarding. I am well aware that my periodic feelings of self-doubt from childhood to today are born out of my own insecurities. I'm glad for some of those awkward moments. If nothing else, they remind me to not take myself so seriously.

PAUSE TO PONDER

> Looking back on your own life, you have likely experienced times when you felt a bit out of place. Some situations may have been difficult, but surely there were at least one or two that now make you laugh. What was your most laughable moment? What is one positive outcome you gained from the experience?

Every human heart longs to be accepted, to be loved—to *belong*. This is evident in many of the stories we have been studying over the past six weeks.

- We saw it in the life of Jacob, who went so far as to disguise himself as his father's favored son in order to obtain his father's blessing.
- We saw it in the life of Leah, who hoped that producing children would earn her husband's love.
- We saw it in the life of Judah, who was so jealous of his father's favoritism that he was willing to sell his own brother into slavery.
- We saw it in the life of Tamar, who was desperate enough to degrade herself in order to secure a place in Judah's family.

> No human being can ever fill the spiritual hole in our heart—but God can.

> "I have blotted out your transgressions like a cloud and your sins like mist; return to me, for I have redeemed you."
>
> —Isaiah 44:22

What was true then is still true today. Everywhere we look, there are souls yearning for love, yearning to belong. From the time sin entered our world, each of us has been longing to fill the spiritual hole in our heart. No matter how hard we try or how hard we look, no human being—whether a child, spouse, parent, or anyone else—can ever fill that hole.

But God can.

God Made a Way

Read Isaiah 44:22 in the margin.[13] What comes to mind when you hear the word *redeem* or *redemption*? How would you describe it?

Look up *redemption* in a Bible dictionary or a standard dictionary. Rewrite the definition using your own words.

Compare your definition with the one in the dictionary. Are they the same or different? Explain.

Read Ephesians 1:7-10 in your Bible. Fill in the missing words from verse 7, printed below (copied from the New King James Version).

In Him we have _____ through His blood, the _____ of sins, according to the riches of His grace.

What did your redemption cost?

What did it accomplish?

Day Five / Week Six

Why does it matter? What difference has redemption made:

In your life personally? Be specific.

⮕ In the world? (Hint: imagine a world where God's redemption does *not* exist.)

One of my favorite passages of Scripture is Ephesians 1. The entire chapter bursts with the incredible promises God lavishes on His beloved children—not because of anything we have done, but because of what Christ has done for us.

Yesterday, we looked at verses 3–6, including the beautiful fact that believers are adopted into God's family. Then, in the previous exercise, we looked at verses 7–10, where we focused on the glorious redemption that is ours through the precious blood of Christ. Praise Jesus that through His sacrifice for sin, we are no longer children of wrath (Eph. 2:1–3) but children of God!

Wait, there's more!

Bearing the Mark of God's Image

Read Ephesians 1:11-14. Fill in the missing words from verses 13-14, printed below (copied from the English Standard Version).

In him you also, when you heard the word of truth, the gospel of your salvation, and believed in him, were _____ with the promised Holy Spirit, who is the _____ of our _____.

In your Bible, highlight or mark each occurrence of the phrase "in him" (or "in Christ" or equivalent) in Ephesians 1:3-14. (Note: some paraphrase versions of the Bible may not work for this exercise.)

How many "in him" assurances did you discover?

Of these, which one do you need most in your life right now? Explain.

If God's love and redemption and all that comes with it were not already enough, through Christ we have been given an incredible gift: we are sealed by the Holy Spirit of God.

Recall from Week Four: What is the purpose of a signet or seal? Circle the word that best completes the sentence below. Then, use the word to fill in the blank. (Hint: see the section "Stolen Identity" in Day Four of Week Four.)

deposit   purchase   ownership   artistic ability

Like a fingerprint, the signet would leave a unique seal (imprint) providing proof of _____ on his possessions.

Being sealed by God's Holy Spirit means that we have God's Holy Spirit living within us (2 Cor. 1:22). It also means that, spiritually speaking, we bear the mark of His image.

Write Romans 8:29 below.

> "God . . . has also put his seal on us and given us his Spirit in our hearts as a guarantee."
> —2 Corinthians 1:22

Let's be honest. Being conformed to the image of the Son of God is a tall order. On our own, it is impossible. It is also a process, one that begins the moment we are "born again" as children of God and continues until it is perfected on the day we enter glory (1 John 3:2). This spiritual transformation is only possible because God has graciously given His own Holy Spirit to live within us (Titus 3:5–6).

PAUSE TO PONDER

Think back on the past month. When it comes to living a life pleasing to God, on which side of the spectrum do you tend to lean: your own efforts or the Holy Spirit? Mark an X on the line below.

my own efforts   the Holy Spirit

What area in your life right now are you leaning more on your own efforts? What would it look like if you were to lean on the Holy Spirit in this area? What one step will you take in that direction?

Our Hope of Heaven

As believers, you and I have the joy and comfort of knowing God's Holy Spirit will never leave us (John 14:15–18). Even more, Ephesians 1:14 says His Spirit is given to us as a guarantee of an inheritance still to come. The rich truths packed into this one verse come to light when we pause to examine the original language. The Greek word translated *guarantee* (*arrabon*) is borrowed directly from Old Testament Hebrew. The first time the word appears in the Bible is when Tamar asks Judah for a pledge. In Genesis 38:17, the Hebrew word for *pledge* is *erabon*.

> Reflect back on the story of Judah and Tamar; what payment did Judah promise to send, and what pledge did Tamar request? (Hint: see Gen. 38:17-18.)

> Apart from Tamar's obvious aim of conceiving Judah's child, what else could Tamar have been seeking? What "hole" might she have been trying to fill? List two or three possibilities.

As we know, Tamar never returned to retrieve the goat Judah promised. In the end, Tamar was not looking for a fee, but a family—a ticket back into Judah's home and, ultimately, a place in the family genealogy. In short, Tamar sought a place where she would belong. In an earthly sense, God blessed Tamar with just that. But God is a lavish God. In His grace, He does so much more! Why? It turns out that God and Tamar share something in common. God also desires a family—a people to call His own. God does not need us, but He takes holy pleasure in lavishing His love on His beloved children. Did He choose Tamar because she was deserving? Righteous? Faultless? No. In fact, God seems to enjoy doing the opposite (1 Cor. 1:26–31). The reality is that if any of us could come to Him based on our own merits or goodness, there would be no need for redemption.

In love, God chose to redeem Tamar for His own glory—along with Jacob and Judah and Ruth and Rahab and countless others broken by sin since the days of Adam—redeemed not because of anything they had done, but because of what

Christ did for them. In love, He grafted them, along with all who put their trust in Him, into His own family. If you are a child of God, there is an inheritance "kept in heaven for you" (1 Pet. 1:4). *An inheritance!* And the only thing you need to receive it is to belong to the One who owns it all.

> *Fear not, for I have redeemed you;*
> *I have called you by name, you are mine.*
> Isaiah 43:1b

YOUR TURN

Every generation has its heroes—from ancient times until this very day. Yet even the best ultimately fall short. Their stories stir our hearts' longing for a hero who never disappoints, who never caves to sin. We need more than a hero; we need a Savior. Praise God that where everyone else falls short, Jesus rises up. Because Jesus is both fully God (Col. 1:19) and fully man (John 1:14; Rom. 1:3–4), He alone can fulfill every aspect of God's redemptive plan.

- God set Adam over creation and then pushed the reset button with Noah in a type of re-creation, but Jesus ushered in a new creation. (2 Cor. 5:17; Rev. 21:1, 5)
- God instituted a covenant[14] and sacrificial system through Moses, but through Jesus's full and final sacrifice for sin, we enter into a new covenant. (Heb. 9:15)
- God promised a national king through Judah and anointed David to rule His people, but Jesus is the King of kings to whom every knee will bow. (Rev. 19:16)

Jesus is the hero every human heart is longing for, the "seed of the woman" God promised from the beginning. For reasons known only in the mind of God, He invited Tamar into His plan of redemption. Tamar could never have imagined that her name would be etched in God's holy Word, much less as an ancestor to the Savior of the world. But even this honor paled in comparison to the joy she experienced the moment she entered eternity and discovered that God had been preparing a place for her all along.

In the same way, if you belong to Jesus Christ, your name has been written in heaven from eternity past, purchased by the blood of Christ, and nothing you have ever done or will do can alter that fact. Throughout the generations of man, God has been setting apart a people to call His own—in His grace, He called you.

> "Rejoice that your names are written in heaven."
> —Luke 10:20

Lesson Summary

What scripture, statement, or thought was most significant to you this week?*
Write it down, and reword it into a prayer of response to God.

*Share your favorite takeaway with a friend or on social media using #TamarBibleStudy. A worship song that celebrates our true hero, Savior, and king is "Great Things (Hero of Heaven)," by Phil Wickham.

Notes

[1] See Gen. 45:6.

[2] See Gen. 43:32, 46:34, and Exodus 8:26. Nevertheless, exceptions did occur, such as the Pharaoh (king) of Egypt attempting to take Abraham's wife Sarai (Gen. 12:10–20) and a later Pharaoh giving Joseph an Egyptian wife (Gen. 41:45).

[3] In biblical times, children were often weaned as late as two to three years old.

[4] Nahum M. Sarna, *The JPS Torah Commentary: Genesis* (Philadelphia: Jewish Publication Society, 1989), 315.

[5] God made a promise to Abraham that "kings will come" from him (Gen. 17:6). The prophecy over his great-grandson Judah is more specific in that it refers to Israel's king who would rule forever.

[6] N. T. Parker and Amy L. Balogh, "Redeemer," in *Lexham Bible Dictionary*, ed. John D. Barry et al. (Bellingham, WA: Lexham Press, 2016).

[7] Tamara Cohn Eskenazi and Tikva Frymer-Kensky, *The JPS Bible Commentary: Ruth*, 1st ed. (Philadelphia: Jewish Publication Society, 2011), 85.

[8] Stan Norman, "Adoption," in *Holman Illustrated Bible Dictionary*, ed. Chad Brand et al. (Nashville: Holman Bible Publishers, 2003), 29.

[9] Or "adoption to sonship," as translated by the NIV. Some translations, such as KJV, translate the word "adoption as children" in order to convey its spiritual application to all believers; however, the literal translation is "adoption as sons" based on the practices of adoption at that time, which involved assigning an adult male as legal heir to one's property.

[10] W. E. Vine, Merrill F. Unger, and William White Jr., *Vine's Complete Expository Dictionary of Old and New Testament Words* (Nashville: Thomas Nelson, 1996), 13–14.

[11] However when it comes to God's people, Scripture includes at least two Old Testament examples where daughters are included in their father's inheritance. During the time of Moses, God established a law granting a daughter inheritance rights if her father had no son (Num. 27:8). See also Job 42:12–15 and Num. 27:1–11.

[12] The words *raised* and *seated* in Ephesians 2:6 are written in a Greek verb form called aorist active indicative. The use of the indicative mood by the author means that the author is making a statement of fact.

[13] Like the passage we explored in Isaiah 54, Isaiah 44 was written in the context of God's relationship to Israel; nevertheless, there are general principles that also apply to all who belong to Him (see Isa. 43:6–7).

[14] God made various covenants with His people (for example, Noah, Abraham, and David), but through Moses, God established the law and sacrificial system which became obsolete when Jesus offered Himself as a sacrifice for sin once and for all (Exod. 19–24; Heb. 9–10).

Genealogy of Jesus Christ

The firstborn among many brothers.

Romans 8:29

Firstborn	Chosen[1]
_____	
Eliab	_____
Er	_____
Reuben	_____
Esau	_____
Ishmael	_____
	_____
	_____
Cain	_____
Adam	

The righteous flourish like the palm tree.

Psalm 92:12a

---

[1] "Chosen," as it is used here, relates to Jesus's human ancestral line.

NOTES

NOTES

NOTES

NOTES

Don't miss the first study in the Behind the Seen series!

HAGAR
Rediscovering the God Who Sees Me

Shadia Hrichi

ISBN 978-0-89112-470-2

Witness the depths of God's compassion through the eyes of a runaway slave.
How much do we really know about the young slave girl Hagar? She is often relegated to the backstage as a minor character in God's redemptive story. But was she? Do you know how her story ends? Rest assured that it does not end in despair. In fact, she emerges victorious! Through this seven-week, in-depth Bible study, you will find that when you surrender your life into God's hands, your trials and triumphs serve a magnificent purpose: to draw you into the arms of the faithful *God Who Sees Me*.

"Deep and packed with surprising insights! I enjoyed exploring the story of Hagar—an often-discarded woman who played a profound part in human history.... This study beautifully captures the depth of God's love for all people. I am excited to share it with others!"
   —**Francine Rivers,** international best-selling author

"This study is a personal and compelling guide to a powerful and under-appreciated story of God's faithfulness."
   —***Bible Study Magazine,*** a publication of Faithlife, the creator of Logos Bible Software

Visit shadiahrichi.com for updates on new books and resources in the Behind the Seen series.

The second study in the Behind the Seen series!

LEGION

Rediscovering the God Who Rescues Me

Shadia Hrichi

ISBN 978-1-68426-370-7

Tormented, chained, and living in a graveyard, the man known only by the name of the demons that tormented him had no one to help him—no one to intercede for him. No one but Jesus. Climb into the boat with Jesus as He heads into enemy territory. Witness Jesus's power and passion as He battles violent storms and armies of demons to rescue . . . one . . . lost . . . soul.

Through this six-week, action-packed study, you will experience God's relentless love as you celebrate the impassioned Savior Who moved heaven and earth to rescue you.

"Shadia has written another outstanding study. *Legion* is rich and in-depth. There were so many new insights; several brought tears to my eyes. Well written and well organized, this study is packed with valuable life lessons. I can't wait to read the next one!"
    —**Francine Rivers,** international best-selling author

"Though one of the more obscure individuals to experience Christ's powerful rescuing love, this man's life is destined to become a much loved Bible story as Shadia leads you into his broken world. I highly recommend this stunning, thorough, unforgettable, hope-filled Bible study."
    —**Dr. Phyllis Bennett,** director of the Women's Center for Ministry at Western Seminary

Visit shadiahrichi.com for updates on new books and resources in the Behind the Seen series.

www.ingramcontent.com/pod-product-compliance
Lightning Source LLC
LaVergne TN
LVHW080305260326
834688LV00039B/1146